The Chelsea Flower Show

Hester Marsden-Smedley

THE CHELSEA
FLOWER SHOW

Constable London

First published in Great Britain 1976
by Constable and Company Limited
10 Orange Street London WC2H 7EG
Copyright © 1976 by Hester Marsden-Smedley
All rights reserved

ISBN 0 09 461090 8

Set in Monotype Garamond
Printed in Great Britain by The Anchor Press Ltd
and bound by Wm Brendon & Son Ltd
both of Tiptree, Essex

For
Anne Pinney and Sue Marsden-Smedley
Gardeners in two hemispheres

Acknowledgements

I have lived in Chelsea for forty-nine years, and had the privilege of knowing many of its famous citizens, whose memories and reminiscences go back even further. It is to these men and women, some long dead, who knew and loved Chelsea the place, and to others who knew and loved Chelsea the Flower Show, that I owe my greatest debt of gratitude.

I want to thank the Royal Horticultural Society, to which the Chelsea Show owes its inception and continued glorious existence. I am afraid that I cannot list all the names of Council members, staff and Fellows who have helped me in innumerable ways and shown such patience, but I want especially to thank Miss Elspeth Napier (Editor of the RHS *Journal*, now the *Garden*) Mr P. F. M. Stageman, Librarian at Vincent Square, Mr R. T. Scase, Librarian at Wisley and their staffs. Admiring thanks also go to Mr T. Sargent of the Shows Office.

I am indebted to the Society's historian for the delight as well as the information in his book *The Story of the Royal Horticultural Society, 1804–1968* (OUP 1969).

General Sir Antony Read, GCB, CB, DSO, MC, Governor of the Royal Hospital and members of his

6

staff have been most helpful. Also the recently retired Superintendent of the Grounds, Edward Sweeting, whose knowledge and experience of Shows over many years was invaluable. I want to thank Mr W. S. S. Breem of the Inner Temple Library, the staff at Chelsea Public Library (including the late Librarian Mr Cyril Edwards) and in particular Mrs Pratt and Mrs Downs of the Reference Library. Also Mr Allen Paterson of the Chelsea Physic Garden.

I could not even have begun this work without the help of the *Gardener's Chronicle*. I thank the Editor and his staff. Mr Roger Newman, its News Editor, gave me much needed encouragement from the first.

I am very grateful to the Agricultural Ministries and Embassies of several countries who have supplied information. Particular thanks are due to M Meurice Cammaerts, the Belgian Agricultural Attaché, for research into the early days of the 'Floralies' at Ghent.

Mr F. G. Potter, VMH, of Messrs Suttons bravely lent me his original print of a vegetable display at the 1913 Show – the first – and Mr Louis Russell of L. R. Russell lent some attractive pictures. I would like to thank them both.

Very warm thanks are due to two men who have given eyewitness accounts. Mr C. C. Titchmarsh wrote an article for the *RHS Garden Club Journal* about the Royal International Horticultural Exhibition of 1912. Mr C. Bartlett's vivid description of the Jubilee Exhibit from Exbury in 1935 was written specially for me.

Many individuals, firms, organizations and institutions are named in the text. I want to thank them all for their co-operation. I would specially mention Mr L. P. Avery of Town and County Catering. Also the manager of the Victoria Branch of the National Westminster Bank and his staff.

I have corresponded with many people and talked with more while preparing this book and to all I give my thanks. Lastly, among personal friends who have been untiring in giving me time and ideas and helping with research, typing and transport, I would affectionately thank Miss Julia Clements, Mr Edward Goldring, Miss Sarah Lumley-Smith, Mrs Nesta Macdonald, Mrs Mary Pope, Mrs Sue Westbrook and Lady Villiers.

Illustrations

The Royal Hospital (*Aerofilms Ltd*)   frontispiece

(*Colour*) *between pages 20 and 21*
Camellia in a willow-pattern bowl (*Suttons*)
Water enhances beauty (Rochford's exhibit, 1973.
  Print by Downward)
Roses around the obelisk (John Mattock 1975.
  Print by Downward)
A carpet of colour (*Suttons*)

(*Black and White*) *between pages 36 and 37*
Vegetables displayed at the first Show, 1913 (*Suttons*)
Tulips – a spring flower for a spring show (*RHS*)
King George V and Queen Mary (*RHS*)
The rock-gardens (*RHS*)
Stepping stones (*RHS*)

between pages 76 and 77
The nineteen-twenties (*Russell*)
Laying out a water-garden (*RHS*)
An all-too-familiar scene (*RHS*)
Summerhouses (*RHS*)

Staking plants (*Suttons*)
Crowds at the Show (*RHS*)
Trophies and medals (*RHS*)
The important task of judging (*John Bignell*)
Garden path in a marquee (*Suttons*)
Queen Mary at the Artists' tent (*RHS*)
Succulents (cacti) (*RHS*)
An exhibit from Wisley (*RHS*)
The way to a perfect lawn (*Suttons*)
A woodland garden (*Russell*)

between pages 116 and 117
The Queen Mother enjoys a strawberry
   (*Press Association*)
A pensioner at the Show (*Fox Photos*)
The Constance Spry Stand, 1954 (*Cowderoy and Moss*)
A gold medal for vegetables (*Fox Photos*)
Roses: a 1973 exhibit (*Downward*)
Her Majesty the Queen and Prince Philip (*Fox Photos*)

1

To many people the world over, the name 'Chelsea' means, not a London borough, but the few days each year when British horticulture is there in all its splendour. The great marquee in the Royal Hospital grounds is ablaze with colour, crammed with gardeners old and young, and fragrant with flower-scents sweet and spicy, and with the rich, damp smell of earth. Great banks of brilliant tulips, together with massed daffodils, true Spring flowers, signify that this is the Royal Horticultural Society's Great Spring Show. But it is a show for all seasons, for there are also roses in abundance, delicate sweet-peas, bold blue-purple delphiniums and all the dazzling herbaceous plants of summer. Autumn tints are there in all the heathers, and winter is foreseen and cheerfulness promised in flower arrangement displays, and, of course, the evergreens.

Orchids, in exotic unearthly shapes and colours, are generally on their own, and are among the most outstanding features of the Chelsea Shows. They are also security risks – in earlier days cultivators would use a fine brush to remove every trace of pollen, the gold dust of years of careful breeding. Some still do, but security is tighter now and grows more so each year. Rhododendrons and azaleas are much admired, and displays increase yearly, many coming from very far places, the result of special collectors' travel. Hybrids from early discoveries are both interesting and beautiful.

Vegetables and fruits are perfectly arranged in patterns and pyramids, almost as beautiful as flowers. The scarlet strawberries are a security risk second only to the orchids – though for reasons of greed, not profit.

Outside, whatever the weather, whatever the day or hour, the queue for admission at the London Gate winds away down Royal Hospital Road. Once inside, crowds mill round the stands on the tree-lined Avenue: stands displaying tools and machines, fertilizers and pesticides, greenhouses and garden chairs, books and magazines. There are florists' displays, a First-Aid post and information bureaux: the most important of these is set up by the Royal Horticultural Society itself, with staff from its garden at Wisley ready to answer questions. But visitors often ask horticultural advice of clerks at the Bank and Post Office as well.

The practical side of gardening is much in evidence. Information at hand ranges from soil clearance, through every scientific aspect of propagation and cultivation, to the problems of exporting and importing plants. But most people come simply for the joy of it, to admire and envy, to be inspired by visions of perfection, to be overcome by the richness of colour and scent.

The Chelsea Spring Show, as it now is, began in May 1913, and with the exception of a few war years has continued ever since. Behind the Show lies the dedicated creative work of the Royal Horticultural Society (which hereafter will be referred to by its initials – RHS), as well as the co-operation of the authorities at the Royal Hospital, in whose lovely grounds the Show is held.

Layout has changed over the years, familiar names have disappeared and new names have become established in their turn, but the Show's unchanging factor, and to many its greatest charm, is the faithfulness and affection of all its supporters – exhibitors and visitors alike.

The Show covers about twenty-three acres of the Royal Hospital grounds. More than two weeks is needed for preparations immediately before opening, but planning for the next year begins even before the current Show is finished. Yet so perfected have the arrangements become, after more than fifty years' experience, that the occasion has a lighthearted atmosphere which neither the weather nor political or economic upheavals can destroy.

The Royal Hospital, rich in history, stands beside the Thames, with magnificent buildings designed mainly by Sir Christopher Wren. Visitors entering by the London Gate can see Lighthorse Court on the right; while on the left are offices of the Royal Hospital, behind which are new buildings replacing those destroyed by bombardment in 1941.

The great marquee is the centre of the Show. It covers

some three and a half acres, and is a masterly piece of skilled construction by the firm of Piggott Brothers of Ongar. The breathtaking displays inside are mostly arranged by individual firms or nurseries, and vary in size and design. Commonwealth and foreign countries have sent displays since the Spring Show's forerunner, the Royal International Horticultural Exhibition of 1912. Belgium and Holland are among the most regular exhibitors – Belgium, with its superb 'Floralies' of Ghent, have been leaders in horticulture for decades. France and Germany have contributed from time to time. Japanese stands, with their graceful economy of design, have long been a feature: the tiny and exquisite Bonzai trees, many of which are now grown in this country, are always favourites.

Beyond the marquee, near the entrance on the Embankment (at what is known as the Bull Ring), there are rock and water gardens, favourites from the first. In the early years some were sold as they stood, and were transported stone by stone to country houses, or gardens abroad.

There are separate enclosures, where the President of the RHS entertains Royalty on the day before the opening, and where distinguished visitors are received. In the sector for the general public there are seats for rest and refreshment areas of various kinds at different prices. The alteration in these over the years is in itself an interesting sign of social change.

Judging takes place on Monday, before the Show opens, and the Award certificates make their appearance on the winners' stands before the visitors arrive. The Private View for Fellows and their friends is on the Tuesday, differing from many a fashionable Private View at London art galleries, in that the exhibits are looked at first and foremost, and famous and freakish visitors come second.

The next three days the Show is open to the public, at varying prices. During this period there are lectures, demonstrations and horticultural committee meetings. There are informal meetings, too, of fellow enthusiasts from all over the country, for the Chelsea Flower Show is a welcome meeting-place for old friends. One Fellow of the RHS said that if it were not for the Flower Show, he would hardly see anyone living outside a few miles' radius of his Yorkshire home, from one year's end to another.

On the last day, a Friday, many plants are sold, and the pavements are full of people, dwarfed by the flowers and bushes they are carrying, hurrying home with their spoils for London gardens. (The term 'cash and carry' is said to have originated at the Chelsea Flower Show.) I know of many plants in Chelsea which came from different Shows – I have a clematis carried home in 1937, since transplanted but still in fine health, cuttings from which grow in the gardens of family and friends. Fine fuchsias and hydrangeas beautify the yards of Council Estates nearby. Chelsea's rich earth encourages gardeners as it has done down the centuries, in spite of modern bulldozers and concrete. I remember one year a lupin bravely pushing up through the nearby tarmac.

As a neighbourhood, Chelsea has always been famous for its gardens. Grapes from Chelsea once provided the Abbot of Westminster with his wine; vines still grow locally and bear fruit. Thomas More planned a garden running down to the Thames, where he walked with his friends among his plants, some mentioned in *Utopia*. His good friend King Henry VIII walked with him, his arm around More's neck – the neck severed by the King's order not so very long afterwards. Mulberry trees, loaded with fruit, still grow in Chelsea as they grew in the fifteenth-century gardens of the Manor House where King Henry's daughter, the young Princess Elizabeth, used to play.

Gardening references to Chelsea abound through the ages. Narcissus Luttrell cultivated twenty-five varieties of pear in the garden of Shaftesbury House (where St Stephen's Hospital now is) between the years 1712 and 1717. A descendant of his read a paper to the RHS on this remarkable achievement.

In 1777, 'Capability' Brown laid out a garden for Henry Holland, architect of much of Hans Town, the area round Sloane Street. The house is said to have resembled the Brighton Pavilion: no trace of colonnaded house or fine garden remain, but Pavilion Road runs north alongside Sloane Street from Sloane Square.

The first moss rose was allegedly produced in Chelsea, by Mr Shailer, a lavender grower near Upper Cheyne Row. Mrs Banks, mother of Sir Joseph Banks, botanist and explorer, lived in Turret House, almost next door to the Royal Hospital, but long since pulled down. Banks spent much of his youth in Chelsea, fishing in the Thames: as an adult he voyaged with Captain Cook and was one of the seven founders of the RHS. On his voyage to Australia he saw the flowering plant locally known as honeysuckle, which now bears his name (*Banksia*) and which is now also grown in this country. The Banksian medal for plants of merit presented at RHS meetings (as opposed to papers which were read there) was instituted in 1820.

The greatest garden in Chelsea is undoubtedly the Physic Garden, lying along the river to the west of the Royal Hospital, the second oldest Botanical Garden in the country. First mentioned in a deed of 1647 as 'all those three parcels of arable land . . . abutting on the river', it was bought in 1673 by the Apothecaries' Company, and the year after that the land was walled and herbs planted. The terms of its lease state that the garden should be for the 'manifestation of the power, wisdom and glory of God in the works of Creation', and such its purpose still remains.

Its fame really began when Sir Hans Sloane bought the Manor of Chelsea in 1722, and conveyed the garden to the Society of Apothecaries in perpetuity. Sloane's statue by Rysbrack stands in the centre of the garden today. He was an ardent naturalist and collector – his vast collection of rarities and oddities formed the basis on which the British Museum was founded. As a young man he had travelled widely as a doctor, and had visited many West Indian Islands as physician to the Governor of Jamaica: two huge illustrated volumes by Hans Sloane, called *Natural History of Jamaica*, have many detailed and fascinating botanical plates.

There is a twentieth-century echo of this. In 1913, the year of the first Chelsea Show, Sydney Olivier was appointed Secretary to the Board of Agriculture. He had previously been Governor of Jamaica and was the proud possessor of Hans Sloane's books about that island. He said he hoped that, centuries later, those inspiring botanical researches would help guide him in his new post.

Until 1770 Philip Miller, that 'prince of Gardeners', was Curator of the Physic Garden; his monumental work, *The Gardener's Dictionary*, was first published in 1731, though the eighth edition of 1768 is the one most frequently used. The *Dictionary* owed an immense amount to Miller's work and researches in the Physic Garden. In 1731 there were about a thousand plants there; plants from foreign climates and countries were being collected and knowledge was increasing about their needs and cultivation. By the time Miller died, in 1771, the number of plants had increased to five thousand, and interest in them was spreading, for Miller delighted in passing on information to 'curious delighters in flowers' – his name for those who grew rare plants.

Miller had many pupils, among them Elizabeth Blackwell, author of *A Curious Herbal*, which contained five hundred of the plants most useful to the practice of medicine. She worked very hard on this book, illustrating it herself from drawings made in the Physic Garden, opposite which she had lodgings. She then engraved and coloured the plates, spurred on not only by a love of the subject but by the need to raise money to free her husband Alexander from a debtors' prison. She succeeded, but his wild life continued; and nothing is heard of this devoted and talented wife after the publication of her *Herbal* in 1737.

Today the Physic Garden, not open to the public, no longer concentrates on purely medical plants. Its work is largely botanical, and more than 30,000 specimens are sent every year to schools and colleges for study.

As exquisite, in their way, as Elizabeth Blackwell's engravings, were the flowers and plants on the porcelain produced at the Chelsea China Works, in Lawrence Street, from 1745 until 1770. Many of the plants – more properly, botanic displays with remarkably accurate reproductions of leaves, stems and fruit as well as flowers – were copied direct from the illustrations in Philip Miller's *Gardener's Dictionary*; and these patterns on plates and dishes are known as Hans Sloane Flowers to this day – presumably because of Sloane's close connection with the Physic Garden and his interest in the China Works. Her Majesty, Queen Elizabeth the Queen Mother, has a fine collection of Hans Sloane plates.

There is another link between Chelsea china and gardening: about 1769 the great potter, Josiah Wedgwood, sent down from Staffordshire some ware to be decorated in Chelsea, at an establishment run by Wedgwood's friend and partner, Thomas Bentley. Josiah's third son John, born in 1766, was destined to become a founder member, and the first treasurer, of the Horticultural Society.

Other early and prominent members of the Horticultural Society had particular links with Chelsea too. Richard Anthony Salisbury (1761–1829) was one of the seven founder members and its second Honorary Secretary. He was born Markham, son of a Leeds cloth merchant, and took the name Salisbury on the death of his cousin, Miss Anna Salisbury, from whom he received a large legacy. The money enabled him to complete his studies at Edinburgh University, and to found botanic gardens – in 1807 he bought about six acres in Chelsea near Sloane Street, laying them out in the Linnean tradition. These gardens changed hands many times over the years, and later became a public promenade. Later still, Cadogan Place was built on part of the site, and Messrs Waterer's famous Rhododendron Show was held there for years.

While Salisbury owned this ground, he was helped by Joseph Knight (1781–1855) who had a very great part, horticulturally, to play in Chelsea. He came of very humble origins in Lancashire, and began life as a garden boy, soon coming to London to work with George Hibbert of Clapham, a keen amateur botanist and one of the earliest members of the Horticultural Society. Later Knight moved across the river to hard but profitable work in Chelsea with Salisbury. He was essentially a gardener with little scientific knowledge, but with a great love of plants and a real flair for business. He did, however, publish a technical botanical treatise, probably based on Mr Salisbury's work and dedicated to Mr Hibbert.

It was with Mr Hibbert's help – and also with his plants – that Joseph Knight founded his Nursery Garden, to the south of the King's Road, not far from Chelsea's western boundary. This remarkably successful nursery, first known as Mr Knight's Royal Exotic Nurseries, helped finance his charitable projects – one of these was the purchase made by Knight and Mr Salisbury (both Roman Catholics) of a strip of land south of Cadogan Street, to be reserved for a church, Convent school and almshouses. On this strip of land stand St Mary's Church, school and almshouses today.

Knight's nurseries later became known as Knight and Perry's, and finally as Veitch's. The name Veitch is

famous in the horticultural world – though like many a good prophet, he is perhaps less honoured in his own neighbourhood than he should be. The Veitch family was of Scottish descent, but John Veitch (1752–1839) came south to Devon and in 1808 founded the Killerton Nurseries near Exeter. His son James (known as 'the younger') came to London to work at a Vauxhall nursery, especially to study orchid growing. In 1853 he and his father bought the nurseries of Knight and Perry, which became, and remained, a Veitch family business until it closed, and was soon built over, in 1914.

The nurseries kept the 'Royal Exotic' title, and exotic plants remained a speciality. But more homely ones were not forgotten; dahlias had been a great interest and success at the Exeter Nursery and remained so in Chelsea. They also produced vegetables: one member of a respected firm of Chelsea greengrocers used to say that the finest products of the great country gardens could not equal that which was grown 'down the King's Road'. A magnificent variety of Cos lettuce grown there bore the name, 'Self-folding Chelsea Imperial'.

The Veitch family were passionate gardeners and botanists. They financed travellers who went around the world in search of specimens: *Hortus Veitchii*, written and published by James H. Veitch in 1906, tells the story of their journeys, their adventures and achievements. The family was soon associated with the Horticultural Society. The Veitch Memorial Medal, instituted in 1870 in admiring memory of James Veitch, who had died a year earlier, is a great honour, bestowed by the Society on those who serve its interests exceptionally well. Gardening talk was a constant feature of life in the Veitch family house in the King's Road Nursery Gardens: it was in their parlour that the idea of forming fruit and floral committees of the RHS was first discussed.

Sir Harry Veitch, knighted in 1912, was the last of this great family of horticulturalists. I remember seeing him once, with his long white beard, still fresh complexion, and very proud of his 'gardener's hands'. He seemed to have the spirit of eternal vigour, becoming an excellent Treasurer of the RHS at the age of seventy-eight. His influence and inspiration is still felt.

But among the many sites and people particularly connected with gardening in Chelsea, none is more illustrious than the Royal Hospital grounds, home of the Chelsea Flower Show each year. Famous pleasure gardens stood here in the eighteenth century, in the grounds of Ranelagh House. They are long gone, but accounts of the splendid festivities held there can be read in the diaries of Horace Walpole and the novels of Tobias Smollett. The entertainments were public and very merry: indeed, breakfasts at eighteenpence a head were eventually forbidden by the government as being detrimental to public morals. In all these entertainments, the well-cared-for flowers and trees were part of the enchantment: the refreshment boxes were roped with fresh flowers, and there were 'festoons of flowers hanging from tree to tree'. Avenues of trees shone with lights: there was music and opera and boating on an artificial lake. Walpole visited it nightly and wrote that it was so fashionable that every step he took, he trod on princes and dukes – though he also said that as well as 'much nobility' there was 'much mob'. A great amphitheatre built in 1748 to celebrate the Peace of Aix-la-Chapelle is described by him in detail:

'The amphitheatre was illuminated; in the centre was a circular bower composed of all kinds of firs in tubs, from twenty to thirty feet high; under them orange-trees with a small lamp in each orange, and below them all sorts of the finest auriculas in pots.'

The Ranelagh Gardens closed in 1804. One of the last functions held there was the Installation Ball of the Order of the Bath in 1802 – rather decorous compared with other rowdier and less distinguished occasions. Then, after years of neglect, when the fine buildings began to fall down, the main part of Ranelagh Gardens was bought for the Royal Hospital, and much of it forms a natural background for the great shows today, with its grounds full of beautiful trees, shrubs and flowers.

The Royal Hospital itself stands where James I had planned a Theological College for the study of 'polemical divinity', which was nicknamed by Bishop Laud 'Controversy College'. Strangely enough, the word 'college' lingers – the scarlet-coated pensioners at the Hospital often use it, and the West Court is called College Court. The Royal Hospital, founded in 1683 for wounded soldiers, was designed by Wren in stately red brick. Alas, the romantic story that the hospital was begun at the instigation of Nell Gwynn has been disproved, but the story lingers on – her portrait hangs in the Great Hall, and she was an early benefactor.

As Wren's magnificent buildings arose, more trees were planted and the gardens were laid out – many for vegetables. The grounds to the south had to be sub-stantially altered when the Embankment was built in

1874. The tall obelisk which Flower Show visitors can see towering above the marquee as they come in at the Embankment entrance was raised to the memory of officers and men of the 24th Regiment who fell at the battle of Chillianwallah, in India.

At the Chelsea Flower Show, town and country come together. It is an important part of what was once the London season, and it is held at what is still the busiest time of London's social year. But, as has been said, it is an informal meeting place too, and it echoes a British tradition of country shows that stretches back through the centuries, a constant in English country life.

Many of these shows began as fairs, or as folk-lore festivals – some derived from far earlier fertility rites. But all were part of what had earned the title of Merrie England. The merriness of England came mainly from the villages, the strength and the life-blood of which was agriculture. In the country everybody has one basic interest, whatever his degree or station, and that basic interest is the earth – whether it be owned, tilled, common-land or private grounds.

The fruits of the harvest formed the centre of any country show, and that included flowers. At Mitcham, bunches of lavender competed against one another; at Pershore Midsummer Fair it was pears. At the once prosperous Charlton Fair in Kent, local people could win prizes for the prettiest flower posies, and the 'Mops' fair at Marlborough had flowers and fruit for display and competition, as well as for sale. They were all part of the great joy of displaying, competing with, and selling the result of, seasonal labours, and the fairs were common up and down the country.

The Victorian era brought more decorum to riotous village customs. The yearly flower shows were usually held in the grounds of the Manor House, probably the only time that these were open to the public. Some lively feast and harvest shows became, as they had once previously been, the prerogative of the Church.

Clare Leighton's delightful illustrated book, *Country Matters* (Gollancz, 1937), in a chapter called 'The Flower Show', has an enchanting description of one such show, with its joys, anxieties and rivalries. The unidentified village where it was held encompassed both hill and valley, and: ' "It ain't no good sending nothing to the Show until they do give us one to ourselves up here on the chalk," old Silas Meadwell would mutter. "Here we do be digging ourselves to death . . . to make something come out of the ground, but there in the plain . . . you ain't needing to do nothing but show your black earth to a seed, and it do sprout before your very eyes." '

Though variety has always been the spice and joy of a Flower Show, the 'one flower' show has become an important occasion also. Early last century there were shows to celebrate the chrysanthemum, the dahlia and the tulip. Stoke Newington in North London is said to have held a show devoted entirely to gooseberries, for the then open land around the New River was famed for its fruit farms. And it was that great rosarian, the Rev Samuel Reynolds Hole, later Dean of Rochester, who determined that there must be a separate show for the queen of flowers. He canvassed and encouraged rose-growers everywhere, and the first Grand National Rose Show was held at St James's Hall, London in July 1858. This was an immense success and was the forerunner of many such shows. It gave impetus to the attention in 1876 of the National Rose Society. The show also caught the attention of cartoonist John Leech, who drew for *Punch* a delightful young lady wearing boxing gloves, and challenging a flowering rose-tree as to 'who is the best girl'.

Gardening clubs, flower guilds and associated societies flourish nearly everywhere, in town and country. In Chelsea, the Chelsea Gardens Guild has members comprising both owners of the few remaining large gardens, and proud possessors of tiny flower-filled areas and window-boxes. Nor can I end without remembering Chelsea trees. Authorities and amenity societies constantly press for their care and they are on the whole well looked after, though some Trees of Heaven were hewn down a decade or so ago, and senseless vandals can outrage even the sturdy London plane. Oakley Street, which runs from the King's Road to Albert Bridge, was among the first London streets to be lined with newly planted trees – an idea which the Prince Consort very much admired, and caused to be copied in Kensington.

To the horticultural glories of the past, then, and to Chelsea's proud history, the Royal Horticultural Society's Great Spring Show adds its own triumphant chapter.

2

The idea of forming a Horticultural Society was first put forward by John Wedgwood (son of the great potter, Josiah) in a letter written in 1801. His correspondent was the gardener of King George II, William Forsyth, whose name lives on vividly in the yellow-flowering shrub named after him. Wedgwood asked Forsyth to mention the idea to Sir Joseph Banks, then President of the Royal Society, and Royal Adviser to the gardens at Kew. He replied in six words: 'I approve very much the idea.'

The three men met soon after this, and for the next three years discussed the project. They canvassed experts for their knowledge, noblemen for their patronage and businessmen for funds. And on 7 March 1804 a meeting was held at Hatchards, the booksellers in Piccadilly, to inaugurate a Society for the Improvement of Horticulture. The seven founder members were John Wedgwood (who, though the youngest, presided at the first meeting), William Aiton, Sir Joseph Banks, James Dickson, William Forsyth, the Hon Charles Greville and Richard Salisbury.

The Society grew steadily, enjoyed years of outstanding success and survived those of despair. Once it was very nearly bankrupt. Its first Charter was granted in 1809; others followed, and in 1861 the word 'Royal' was added to its name. The Society altered its officers and its rules, acquired gardens and other premises, but remained faithful to its original purpose – that of improving horticulture. Today it is world famous, with a membership of more than 67,000 in 1975. Horticultural societies may now be common in many countries, but few, if any, have such a massive national membership or such worldwide international connections.

Among the major achievements of the RHS is its furthering of horticultural knowledge. In 1818 it began an experimental garden in Kensington, thanks chiefly to the impetus of Joseph Sabine, Secretary to the Society from 1816 to 1830. The Society had approached the Physic Garden in Chelsea with this idea in mind, but the Society of Apothecaries had not accepted the suggestion, so one and a half acres of land were rented, at £60 a year, in what today is Kensington High Street, nearly opposite where the Commonwealth Institute now stands. Four years later the Society acquired thirty-three acres at Chiswick, and began work on the large-scale gardens which were to culminate in 1903 at Wisley.

From the early days of the Society it was usual for

Fellows to bring specimens of plants to the meetings, and later competitions were held. These were so popular that in 1883 John Lindley, the famous botanist, suggested holding a larger show under canvas at Chiswick – there was a band, refreshments, and other features of a garden show. Lindley, Secretary to the Society from 1858 to 1863, a some-time lecturer at the Physic Garden and Editor of the *Gardener's Chronicle*, was a very distinguished early member of the Society indeed. The magnificent library at the present headquarters of the RHS in Vincent Square is named after him, for it was his fine collection of books which formed its nucleus. The Lindley medal, founded in his honour, is awarded by the RHS to plants which, among other criteria, 'show exceptional skill in cultivation'. An even wider public can honour John Lindley for really beginning the modern Flower Shows of the RHS which reach their zenith at Chelsea.

In 1888, the RHS arranged with the Benchers of the Inner Temple to hold a show in their grounds between Fleet Street and the River Thames: it was the Society's largest and most ambitious show to date. In spite of many difficulties and almost yearly bad weather, these shows continued until 1911, and in their very success lay the disadvantages that were to force them finally to move. Exhibitors and visitors grew in number every year, and the association with the members and tenants of the Inner Temple became more and more uneasy. Some members felt that any outside function was really a trespass on their legal preserve: even those who were well disposed to the idea found the reality of mud and crowds distasteful. One present-day Bencher remembers his grandfather saying that, delightful though it was to wander between briefs in a lovely garden, there was not really room for dry law and moist plants to be at their best together.

On 3 November 1908 the Inner Temple Bench Minutes record the reading of a letter from the RHS, asking to hold their 1909 Show in May as usual. Considerable discussion arose on this question, and there was evidence of the kind of conflict that still surrounds today's Show – conflict between those who have care of the grounds where the Show is held, and the organizers of the Show itself. That the beautiful lawns of the Temple were threatened by tents and visitors could not completely be compensated for by the knowledge that the whole course of horticulture was helped by the exhibits on show.

In the event, permission was given, but as always, with more restrictions. Among these were: all handbills to be submitted to the Master of the Garden; no advertisements to be fixed to the garden railings or to any buildings of the Inn without consent; the Refreshment Tent to be limited to providing such articles as are usually covered by the term 'Afternoon Tea'. One wonders whether this last referred to a determination to avoid strong drink or strong cooking smells. Stories told by that Bencher's grandfather hint at the latter – he remembers that hot, pungent soups were brewed and sold rapidly in the icy downpours. He also remembers that sherbets, ices and quasi-Oriental concoctions were on sale, and he recalls that sweetmeat wrappers disfigured the dignified grounds.

It was becoming obvious that a move would have to be made. In 1910, permission was again given for the 1911 Show, but the Bench reserved the right to make special regulations nearer the time of the Show. The RHS accepted this reservation, but was already looking out for alternatives.

On 4 November, 1911, a letter was received in the Inner Temple, from the RHS Secretary, the Reverend W. Wilks, which read in part as follows:

'A company has been formed to promote an International Horticultural Exhibition in London in 1912 ... the date fixed for this International Exhibition is May 22–30. In consequence whereof the President and Council have been in consultation with the directors, and have finally consented, at their request, to forgo holding their early summer show in 1912, so as to avoid the possibility of rivalry with the International Exhibition . . . '

The letter continued that the President and Council of the RHS:

'think it only courteous to inform you at the earliest opportunity of the arrangements which they have felt bound to consent to with the directors of the Exhibition, and they hope that nothing may occur in the interval of 1912, on either side to prevent the resumption of the kindly consideration which the Treasurer, Master of the Garden, and Benchers have shown to the Society for so many long years past.'

But when this great International Horticultural Exhibition had come and gone, the future site for the RHS

Spring Show was decided beyond question – and was a timely solution to what had become a serious problem. Later still, on 24 May 1913, when the first real Chelsea Flower Show began, the *Gardener's Chronicle* commented:

> 'It would be ungracious to forget, especially at this moment, the debt of gratitude to the Benchers of the Inner Temple, for generously lending their gardens to the Royal Horticultural Society . . . in the very heart of the Metropolis, upon a site that is rich in historic associations of a kind that must appeal to horticulturalists in general and rosarians in particular.'

(The allusion to rosarians refers to the legend that before the Wars of the Roses began, Lancastrian and Yorkists, arguing in the Temple Gardens, plucked red and white roses respectively from bushes growing there. Roses were certainly their badges, but the dramatic story has little evidence to substantiate it, like so many of our more charming legends. However, a painting of the supposed incident hangs in the Inner Temple Hall, and a large fresco in brilliant colours commemorates it in the House of Commons.)

Although May 1913 was the date of the first Chelsea Show as such, its forerunner the previous year was of major importance. This was the Royal International Horticultural Exhibition, from 22–30 May 1912, for the sake of which the RHS had agreed to cancel its own show that year. The directors of that International Show decided it should be held in the grounds of the Royal Hospital, and the success of their show proved that it was a suitable, as well as a splendid site.

There had been a Flower Show in the Royal Hospital grounds once before – the RHS's own Summer Show, in June 1905. However, this was comparatively small, making little impact compared with the regular RHS Shows in the Temple. It was widely felt by exhibitors and officials alike, that Chelsea was too far from the centre of London. Would people take the trouble to journey there, as they had done to the more accessible Charing Cross for Temple Shows? There was considerable doubt, though Mr Harry Veitch, with his own magnificent nurseries down the King's Road, naturally dismissed any objections based on distance, and held that the Royal Hospital grounds were ideal.

The Royal International Horticultural Exhibition was, therefore, an experiment on a very bold scale. The idea had come from within the RHS, but it had decided to remain discreetly in the background. In the words of the RHS historian, Dr H. R. Fletcher: 'it was thought wise that the Society should act as a benevolent godparent rather than the responsible promoter of the Exhibition . . . ' So a small public company was formed, with twenty-six directors under the presidency of the Duke of Portland.

Chairman of the company organizing this show was J. Gurney Fowler, who was Hon. Treasurer of the RHS, and head of a famous firm of accountants. Gardening was his main hobby, with orchids as his special love – he was also then Chairman of the Orchid Committee of the RHS. 'During the many months of anxious preparation,' wrote the *Gardener's Chronicle Supplement* of May 1912, 'the extraordinary optimism of the Chairman has never failed him for a moment; and his enthusiasm has often inspired his colleagues at moments when some were apt to become doubtful or faint-hearted.'

Difficult and invidious as it would now be to apportion credit for the ideas, organization and remarkable success of this Exhibition, hearsay and private correspondence make it clear that the determination and business skills of Sir Jeremiah Colman, Hon. Treasurer to the company, were an enormous influence. He came of a Norfolk family, but was then living at Gatton Park, near Redhill in Surrey, where his head gardener was Mr B. F. Perfect; and his enthusiasm and love of flowers was a byword. His skill in speaking straightforwardly and clearly may have been partly responsible for the Exhibition's taking place at all – for at a preliminary meeting in the Mansion House in 1911 (presided over by the Lord Mayor, Sir T. Vezey Strong), he made a brilliant but simply stated speech, which comforted the many doubters and spurred on the enthusiasts.

The directors of the company formed to present the Exhibition included working gardeners as well as influential people. This is characteristic of gardening, for in no other profession or industry is there such unity among all concerned. Many directors and managers have never worked on the shop floor, but there can hardly be a horticulturalist, garden lover or seed merchant who does not know how to use a spade. From the first, working gardeners were involved, and among those who were directors of this company was Edwin Beckett, who had

34

been with Lord Aldenham and later with his brother, the Hon. Vicary Gibbs, for many years.

Beckett was an early exponent of artistry in vegetable production, and wrote a book about it: he was also an expert on cooking and preserving vegetables, which increased in importance during the difficult years which followed. Other gardener-directors were A. McKeller, from Windsor Castle; Nicholas Barnes, who had worked at Sandringham but who was then with the Duke of Westminster at Eaton Hall; James Hudson, gardener to Leo de Rothschild at Gunnersbury House; and C. R. Fielder, who combined gardening in Essex with examining for the Public Parks and inspecting gardens for the RHS.

The great horticultural firms were represented, and gave money and services generously. They included A. G. Jackman, whose Woking Nurseries were some of the oldest in the country, and Arthur Sutton, one of the most famous names in the horticultural profession, whose lesser-known interest was tracing the wild origins of garden plants. The then superintendent of Wisley, Mr S. T. Wright, also worked closely with the directors.

Among other directors of the company was Hubert Greenwood of the LCC; C. Harman Payne, who acted as Foreign Press Secretary; R. Hooper Pearson, then Managing Editor of the *Gardener's Chronicle*; and Frederick Janson Hanbury, of the Pharmaceutical Society and the firm Allen and Hanbury. Managing director of the Exhibition was Edward White, a well-known landscape gardener, who was in many ways ahead of his time, and whose artistic appreciation of simplicity was not then always admired.

And, of course, there was also the great Harry J. Veitch. His experience of flower shows was immense: an 'elder statesman' in Belgian horticulture remembers his visits to the famous 'Floralies' of Ghent, where he would not only view the splendid exhibits, but study such details as the texture of pots and how the plants were kept fresh. He had been decorated in Belgium, France and the United States: the Veitch Memorial Fund was founded to commemorate his father, James Veitch; and in 1912, he was knighted by King George V, for his invaluable work on the Royal International Horticultural Exhibition and for his 'continuous services to horticulture'.

It is not easy to determine when the preparations for this Exhibition began, but one thing is evident – publicity was not organized as it would be today. There were constant queries in the Press about this. News of the coming Exhibition had been heard on the grapevine – suitable analogy – some time before there was any official announcement. As late as April 1912, a correspondent from Chew Magna was writing to the *Gardener's Magazine* asking for information about cheap tickets and other facilities. The tart reply was, 'The Directors of the International Exhibition give little information, not taking advantage of the Press.'

However, by 4 May, two and a half weeks before the Exhibition opened, the *Gardener's Magazine* reported that the RHS was now more forthcoming. It was widely publicised that the directors would give privileges to bona fide members of gardeners' mutual improvement societies and suchlike. And, with or without its publicity, the Royal International Horticultural Exhibition was

Vegetables displayed at the first Show, 1913

Tulips – a spring flower for a spring show

*King George V and Queen Mary at the Embankment
Entrance – The Bullring*

(Right)   Preparing the famous rock-gardens

Stepping stones across a rock-garden pool

opened by His Majesty King George V, on 22 May 1912. The attendance exceeded all anticipation.

However, the show was not without its problems. C. C. Titchmarsh, who lives near Bath and who, with the late Walter Cartwright, began his training at Wisley in 1907, wrote a charming short article about its pleasures and confusions, for the RHS *Garden Club Journal*, 1966. He began it, 'Few who took part in the first Chelsea Show now survive,' and today there are even fewer. (Walter Cartwright died suddenly in 1975. Fortunately I had the privilege of meeting him a few days before his death, and hearing his impressions of the 1912 Exhibition.) It is interesting to note that Mr Titchmarsh refers to the *first Chelsea* Show, for that is what the 1912 Royal International Horticultural Exhibition will always be to many people.

Mr Titchmarsh continues:

'Arrangements which were adequate for the Temple Gardens would have been under strain at so great a show, but they would have coped with the problems which arose, had the Society been entirely in charge. Divided responsibilities caused difficulties.

The Society undertook the certification of the new plants and acknowledged the awards as their own. Mr Cartwright will always remember his night-long vigil as he sat receiving the stream of entries. . . . The groups were inspected by juries composed of members of the Society's committees, eminent foreign horticulturalists and other prominent gardeners. These juries were too numerous and too large. I gathered that there was delay in assembling and despatching them, and they were hampered in their tasks by crowds in which gate-crashers were said to predominate. At any rate, the juries enjoyed an extremely good luncheon. The task of checking and recording their awards fell to Mr Gaskell, Assistant Secretary of the RHS, and I was his helper. It soon became apparent that many of the lists were incomplete and some were missing. But under pressure the lists, incomplete as they were, were passed to the confirming authority . . . and were published . . .

Soon we were receiving complaints from exhibitors whose groups had received no award. Well aware that I could easily put my foot in it, I meekly suggested that they enquire of the Secretary, a suggestion they received without enthusiasm.

Many awards were increased and the exhibits which had been missed received their due. We finished very late in the evening. . . . The highlight of our day came at our luncheon, when Mr Fowler drew from a hamper bottles of an outstanding hock, such as I have never drunk since. It was nectar. . . . Even then a few exhibits were missed . . . the final list as published contained a few awards which had not been conferred by eminent gardeners, but by a first year Wisley student. I believe that they were fair.

There were special cups presented by eminent personages, local authorities, societies and newspapers. How they were awarded I do not know. One of these special cups was offered for the best new plant, and there was great competition for it. An American nurseryman was confident that his large Polypodium would win it. He visited us twice daily, and it was

impossible to convince him that we knew nothing
of it . . . '

The late Walter Cartwright added his own vivid impressions, of spending the night receiving entries in the
grounds – of the eeriness, the chill, and of hearing the
dawn chorus for the first and only time in London. He
had little time to view the remarkable exhibits by daylight,
but particularly remembered the little trees, covered with
fruit, brought from Mr Leo de Rothschild's estate at
Gunnersbury. (At the end of the show, all Leo de
Rothschild's fruit and vegetables were presented to
the Royal Hospital pensioners.) From the same fine
garden came the *Primula helodoxa*, which Walter Cartwright said that in all his life he never saw anything to
excel.

One little Chelsea girl, now long since a grandmother,
was taken to the 1912 Exhibition and almost swallowed
up – so she describes it – by the mass of flowers and the
pushing crowds. Her most vivid memory is of fairy-like
Japanese lanterns, lit as dusk fell, which so entranced her
that she walked with her head thrown back to look at
them.

As the name of the Exhibition implied, there were
many displays from abroad – from America, Holland,
France, Germany and Japan. C. C. Titchmarsh writes:
'The only foreign group I clearly recall was that from
Holland, where beautifully arranged baskets of flowers
stood on rather ornate white wooden pillars.' Con-
temporary pundits loudly announced the shape of
exhibits to come, and prophesied the doom of the
English style of displaying growing plants. 'But,' said

Mr Titchmarsh, 'after more than half a century, it is still a long time a-dying.'

A wonderful new rose, which came from France – deep pink with large flowers – won the Gold Cup offered by the *Daily Mail* on the understanding that the winner would be called the *Daily Mail* Rose. It was the first time that a Gold Cup, with fifty guineas as well, had been offered for a single rose. The cultivator was a M. Pernet, who did not like the condition at all, and both Mr Titchfield and Mr Cartwright remembered the ensuing disagreement. M. Pernet and his two sons (both to die in battle a few years later) wanted to call the rose after the wife of the patron of the Pernet family (in particular) and of rose gardens (in general): and a compromise was finally reached which launched this rose on its great career under the name 'Mme Edouard Herriot, the *Daily Mail* Rose'.

Rock gardens occupied the whole length of the Embankment railings. Even for those days, their cost must have been immense, but it was a time when massive rock gardens were in fashion all over the country, and they were rapturously reported in the Press. A campaign was started to secure them as a permanent feature of the London scene, but this was dropped when it was pointed out that they were temporary constructions to display, rather than to grow, plants.

Conferences and lectures were a feature of the Exhibition, and a special tent held a science exhibition, described in the catalogue as being 'arranged to illustrate some of the many points where Science touches Horticulture'. Among the distinguished scientists there, the name of Dr Radclyffe Salaman stands out – his work,

Inheritance in Potatoes was to be of such importance during the two world wars.

Advertisements in the splendidly produced catalogue echo the taste of the age, with garden furniture of ornate Italian design, from stone tables to well-heads; bronze storks from Liberty, and wooden and pottery containers for plants, instead of the ubiquitous plastics of today. Garden tools remain much the same down the years, but fortunately today we have no need for the fierce-looking furnaces essential for the growth of what were then necessarily known as 'Stove Plants'.

Among the glorious real blossoms were astonishingly beautiful artificial flowers made by John Groom's Flower Girls Mission, then in Clerkenwell. A visitor to this 1912 Show remembers a Russian nobleman buying several baskets full; and a descendant of his today owns some of the faded, but still exquisitely realistic blooms.

Music was a feature too, and among the bands playing was that of the 4th Battalion Royal Fusiliers, then stationed at Hounslow. I cannot resist mentioning this, as it had been my father's battalion, and I, as a child, had 'followed the drum' from India to Woolwich, Dublin and elsewhere. I well remember 'Bandsman' E. Wright who conducted, and who sent my father a picture postcard of the Royal Hospital from what he thought an interesting, but unusual, assignment.

As 178,389 people pushed through the turnstiles, fears that Chelsea was too far for visitors to come, vanished. A few went to the Temple in error: strangely enough, it seems that more made that mistake the following year. The Benchers allowed a notice to be fixed to the railings, telling show-goers where to make for and how to get there – including a mention of the nearest hackney stands, horse and motor.

Socially, the Exhibition was a splendid success. C. C. Titchmarsh writes: 'As befitted those spacious days, there was much feasting and entertaining in connection with the Show. I heard of a notable banquet at Vincent Square.' It was not the only one. A large number of guests, invited to the Burford Bridge home of Sir Trevor Lawrence, President of the Council of RHS, travelled by special train from Victoria through the beautiful Surrey countryside to Box Hill. Surrounded by the grounds and shrubberies and plant-houses of Sir Trevor's estate, the guests enjoyed a *déjeuner à la fourchette* – one of the first recorded fork lunches, and an innovation for those still-formal days.

Hospitality was not reserved for the rich and famous: the British Gardeners' Association, with kindly thought for country folk ignorant of London, opened a room at 92 Pimlico Road, near where the Chelsea Barracks now stands, for members and their friends, with rest and refreshment available. There were of course refreshments at the Show itself; apparently these were not limited to items particularly suited to afternoon Tea!

Among other visitors to the Royal International Horticultural Exhibition was Archduke Ferdinand of Austria, travelling incognito with his wife. She was a very keen gardener: a breed of tulip is named after her, and in the grounds of Konopiste Castle, near Prague, flower gardens designed by her can still be seen. C. C. Titchmarsh writes:

'None of us who saw them pass could foresee that a

bare two years later they were to die by an assassin's pistol in faraway Sarajevo. This tragedy was to cause the upheaval which profoundly affected all our lives, and was to bring an end to the era of great private gardens, where wealth and unlimited skilled labour produced the superb examples of cultivation which were such a feature of the Show.'

3

In 1913 a sense of security and prosperity predominated
in Britain, despite industrial disputes, trouble in Ireland
and the public protests of the Suffragettes. (Though one
Suffragette, Miss Ellen Beck, a farmer and horticulturalist in Sussex, declared that they would 'never disturb a
Flower Show'.) At the Annual General Meeting of the
RHS, on 11 February, in the Society's Hall in Vincent
Square, a report was given on the unprecedented success
of the 1912 Exhibition, and an item on the agenda 'The
Great May Show', heralded the future. Completing
twenty-five years as Secretary to the Society (a post he
was to hold for a further three years) was the Reverend
W. Wilks, whose beautiful Surrey gardens in the small
village of Shirley (now absorbed into Croydon) produced

the lovely Shirley poppies, whose fame spread world-wide.

The first RHS Chelsea Show was in sight, and the experience of the previous year showed that earliest possible preparations were needed. The Royal Hospital authorities now realized to what an extent they were committed: there were murmurs of protest, and a few continue to this day. This is not ungenerous or surprising, for, as was seen in the Temple, the delight of some can be the discomfort of others. The Royal Hospital is a national monument of great architectural beauty: the upkeep of splendid buildings is expensive and so is the upkeep of the beautiful grounds they stand in. Besides this, the care of the military veterans, their welfare and comfort and medical needs, is the Royal Hospital's responsibility, and costs money. More is always needed, and the lease of the Royal Hospital grounds to the RHS is a financial help.

In *The Royal Hospital, Chelsea,* by Captain G. C. T. Dean, Captain of the Invalids (Hutchinson, 1950) there appears this comment:

' . . . since 1913 the grounds have had to be let each summer for the Royal Horticultural Society's Show and other purposes. Though popular, these functions necessarily injure the amenities of the Royal Hospital. It may well be asked whether it would not be in the public interest for the Government to make an annual grant so as to avoid the necessity of letting the grounds for show purposes at the best season of the year. . . .'

A few local inhabitants complained about noise –

46

still an annual complaint. There were also protests about traffic, especially from those living nearby. One local dweller remembers her mother saying that she imagined horse droppings would be more speedily removed than was usual, by gardeners exhibiting in the Royal Hospital grounds. Later, anxiety was shown about motor fumes, though no one envisaged how traffic was to build up at Chelsea Flower Show time in the years ahead.

An extra omnibus was put on the route to the Royal Hospital Road, and an extra tram along the lines which then came across Battersea Bridge and continued to the top of Beaufort Street. Arrival by tram was a popular method for the many visiting gardeners of Surrey and Sussex. Their route was: train to Clapham Junction (at that period it claimed to have more trains passing through it than any other station in Europe), tram to the Chelsea side of Battersea Bridge, and then an easy and pleasant stroll along the Embankment, noting the trees and gardens of Cheyne Walk, with possibly an envious glance through the gates of the Physic Garden.

On the whole, the Borough of Chelsea welcomed the advent of the Show. The Mayor of the Borough from 1911 to 1914 was Alderman Frederic Welsh, a revered local citizen and the first Freeman of the Borough. He was a friend of Sir Harry Veitch, and sometimes wore a buttonhole from the Nursery in the King's Road. He never wore an orchid, though these were sometimes pressed on him, saying that they were too exotic for a schoolmaster (which he then was): when Mayor, he protested that with badge and chain they would be too gaudy. He was delighted when it became officially known that the Show was to come to Chelsea, and hoped that it would become part of the Chelsea way of life.

There were, however, complications to this on the civic side. The Royal Hospital stands in Chelsea, and as often as not is called by its name. It is one of Chelsea's finest sights. But it is 'extra-territorial' in a sense, with its own special position and rights. For example, though it is customary for the Mayor of any borough to be the first to welcome visiting Royalty to that borough, and then to present them to whichever leading personage is concerned with the particular occasion, this is not the case at the Royal Hospital. There the Governor always takes precedence by virtue of his position, and it is he who welcomes Royalty, and he who presents the Mayor to them.

In fact, the Mayor of Chelsea was not even invited to the Flower Show in his official capacity until after the Second World War, though many other officials especially connected with public works were guests from the beginning.

Local tradesmen were pleased at the prospect of a large yearly influx of visitors. Hotels were booked out. Restaurants did less well, for the catering at the Show was good. For some years it was in the hands of the firm Searcy Tansley, which had not itself then moved to Chelsea, but which directed operations from Marble Arch. Luncheon menus were printed in French; afternoon teas cost 1s. 2d. A visitor to this 1913 Show remembers that there were Chelsea buns, which she had never tasted before: she was told that they were baked locally. (Indeed, the only true recipe is said still to be in the hands of a family baker in the King's Road.)

The Show staged in 1913 was far smaller than it is

today. It occupied the area between Eastern Avenue and the huge Chillianwallah Monument, which made a fine centrepiece for a floral display, as it has often done since. The Ranelagh Gardens were not used, and only a privileged few were allowed to enter them. The marquee was smaller than today's but there was room enough for an outstanding display of flowers, and a larger-than-ever show of fruit, vegetables and gardening sundries. Though there were new varieties of wistaria, there was criticism in both national and specialist press of the general lack of novelty compared with the 1912 Royal International Horticultural Exhibition. Even the hybrid orchids, wrote the *Gardener's Chronicle*, were less surprising than the *Odontioda* first seen at the Temple in 1904.

However, there was a good deal of praise for the presentation of almost all the exhibits, which looked as natural as flowerbeds in a garden. It may be that this method of staging, which, though changing a little with the times, still keeps a more or less natural appearance, has done more than all else to bring this great Show close to the everyday, amateur gardener. Visitors come to see and admire the glorious specimens, exotic varieties and unusual colours; but they go away feeling that perhaps they too could achieve something on the same lines, no matter how simple their garden.

An enterprising barrow boy did a fine trade on the second day of this 1913 Show with notebooks and well-sharpened pencils. He had been tipped the idea by a contractor's man, he told a sympathizer before he was moved on by the police. In the years that followed, the notebook and pencil have become part and parcel of a Chelsea Show-goer's equipment. Nurserymen and seed merchants provide lists for orders, but there is need for more ordinary notes.

'Put little flowers – saxifrage? like a carpet under bigger things. Something wild-looking near the roses. Mix colours as nearly all flowers go well together. White ones, clumps in lots of places. Don't attempt Canterbury bells, next year they grow leggy . . . '

These are extracts from the notebook of a vistor inspired by the Show in 1913.

The rock gardens that year were as popular as ever: and among the lovely little flowers growing there – alpines, primulas, aubretia – real wild flowers could be seen. These were the delight of a party of children brought from nearby Christchurch School, by their headmaster, Mayor Frederic Welsh. Some of these children, long grown old, have looked in vain for wild flowers in the rock gardens at Chelsea shows today.

Emphasis in the rock gardens was laid on the type of stone used – Derbyshire, limestone, Portland and Swanage stone among many others. Nurserymen and private gardeners would consult the leading geologists of the day, and the geologists in turn visited the Show. One of them remembers particularly how well a rockery of reddish stone, probably Cheddar, showed off the brilliant blue gentians planted there.

Mrs Anne Jewson of Norwich, then a schoolgirl, who accompanied her mother, Mrs Ladell, to the 1913 Show and has not missed one since, remembers of the rock gardens that 'more of them had water displays then than now'. She also recalls how she and her mother would make a beeline for Wallace's iris display, adding to their collection yearly.

An iris garden at a convent in the Midlands was grown from money given to spend at Chelsea. The nuns had a special collecting box for this, among others for more obvious charitable purposes. Later this was done away with as being unsuitable – but the iris garden is there, having been well established through those alms. 'The iris,' said one visitor, 'helps contemplation, more than any other flower.'

Among the vegetable stands, those from Aldenham held pride of place. Edwin Beckett, famous gardener to the Hon. Vicary Gibbs, arranged his wares most artistic-ally – it was rumoured that he polished the white turnips and crimson radishes on his frock coat. That year he was judge of the hardy herbaceous plants, which gave him particular pleasure as he had always loved an herbaceous border. (He used to say that such a border needed more good spadework and less mechanical aid or invention than almost any other feature in a garden.)

Sir Harry Veitch's firm, always original, planted an orchard in the open. It was raided the first evening, as a result of which there was a special meeting of officials and exhibitors to tighten security. It was to be said later of security at Shows, that the Goldsmiths & Silversmiths demanded top security, but that Chelsea ran it a close second.

Prominent among vegetable displays, at this and many later Shows, was that of Messrs Sutton of Reading. For several years these were carried to Chelsea in horse-drawn furniture vans with specially-designed layers inside for the plants. There used to be some dozen vans, and they made

51

the journey in procession. Mrs Jobley, whose parents lived on the high road near Maidenhead, remembers them talking of the passing of what they nicknamed 'Sutton's Circus'.

The band in 1913 was that of the Royal Artillery. Some thought it played too loudly. It was said at the time that Wagner's *Entry of the Gods into Valhalla* almost shook petals from stems and fruit from trees.

By now the Chelsea Show had become an established, and much talked-of, social event. In September 1913 it appeared on stage at Drury Lane, in a play called *Sealed Orders* by Cecil Raleigh and Henry Hamilton, which ran for 115 performances. One scene was set on the Embankment with great posters advertising the Exhibition: another in the big marquee, with the mound of cinerarias round the obelisk and beds of flowers studding the green-covered parterre between great groups of rambler roses. The effect was splendid, although produced of course with artificial blooms, and the play was revived the following year.

The year 1913 ended sadly for the British horticultural world, with the death in December of Sir Trevor Lawrence, President of the RHS for nearly twenty-nine years. He was then eighty-one, and had resigned his office a few weeks before the opening of the 1913 Show, though he still took a great interest in it. He had done much over the years to ensure the success of the RHS Shows, and had taken and implemented the decision to move away from the Temple. Among his talents in the field of literature, art, science and business, was that of making and retaining friends: his obituary in *The Times* recorded that 'he was on terms of close friendship . . .

with Lister, Pasteur, Browning, Meredith, Herbert Spencer . . . ' He was a friend, too, of lesser folk, many of whom remember over the stretch of half a century his unfailing kindness. Sir Trevor was succeeded as President by Field Marshal Lord Grenfell, who held the position for six years, four of which were in war-time.

In the Spring of 1914 an important publication appeared – the *Horticultural Record of the Royal International Horticultural Exhibition of 1912*, dedicated to His Majesty King George V. This not only revived memories of the great Exhibition – which indeed lived on in people's minds for generations – but it encouraged those working on the Show which was to follow shortly. (And encouragement was still needed in those days.) The splendid volume with coloured and half-tone plates then cost £2 2s.: a copy changed hands recently at £75, and that was considered a bargain.

The 1914 Annual General Meeting of the RHS was its 110th, and the large attendance was presided over by Sir Harry Veitch in the absence of the new President. Paragraph 12 of the Society's Report referred to the Chelsea Show: its success in terms of exhibits, attendance and financial results was heartening, but there was, as always, room for improvement. It was decided that this year there should be no raised staging in the big tent, except for the orchids at the far end, where the exquisite sprays could be tabled and set above ground level.

There were also complaints from the exhibitors – 'tempered criticism', the *Gardener's Chronicle* called it. Mr R. W. Wallace of Colchester pointed out that the trade exhibitors deserved high consideration from the Council, as they drew large numbers to Chelsea: and he referred to the restrictions placed on them year after year. Some, he said, were extremely harsh, extremely unfair: for outside exhibitors were forced to put down big deposits before they could set up their stands, and they might well lose these deposits in the end. He hastened to add that these remarks were not made in any 'spirit of antagonism to the success of the Society . . . '

The Chairman explained that they were bound to a large extent by what the authorities of the Royal Hospital demanded of them, and the conditions laid down. When an exhibitor made an exhibit, he said, the deposit was returned; but they had been disappointed a number of times by exhibitors making an entry, getting their name in the catalogue and a certain amount of advertisement, and then not exhibiting. The Royal Hospital authorities, he went on, also complained about the way many exhibitors left the ground, which was often excavated, and not left as it was found. A considerable sum of money was then required to put the ground right. . . .

And so preparations for the 1914 Show continued in a spirit of reasonable amity; and the Show itself justified the efforts made, for, as it drew to a close in brilliant sunshine, takings were greater than in 1913, and the attendance larger than had been the case at the Temple. The press commented favourably on the new method of staging. One reporter wrote:

'The relegation to floor level of all the groups in the great tent except for the end group of orchids must be pronounced a great success. It gives an independence to each and a spaciousness to all, which allows the visitor to imagine himself in a garden and not in a flower shop.'

Fruit and vegetables were slightly down in numbers on previous years. One exhibit came from the Thatcham fruit and vegetable farm near Newbury, which was one of the first – if not the first – horticultural schools exclusively for women. (Miss Beatrix Havergal, famous later for the 'Waterperry Strawberry', was among its scholars.) The Thatcham entry drew this comment from the *Gardener's Magazine* of 30 May 1914: 'Without being disrespectful to the ladies, we venture to think that mere man is not yet outdone in as far as the art of growing and staging vegetables is concerned.'

The 1914 catalogue contained many advertisements which throw light on the different demands of the day, and the way in which they were catered for. Cloches appear more often than formerly, with the claim that amateurs are using the 'truly wonderful invention' with success. Another practical object was Dean's Shreds which were used for nailing climbing plants to the wall, and whose taste sickened insects. (I regret to own that I remember the taste of such shreds when stealing peaches many, many years ago.) There were also many advertisements for apparatus used for sterilizing and bottling fruit, in those far-off pre-freezer days.

The Mendip Nurseries, then managed by Captain Hill, advertised patent slug traps, with smaller versions specially for alpine gardens, price 1s. 6d. When I called at the present Mendip Nurseries (which bear the same name again, after many changes of name and ownership during the intervening years) they knew nothing of these traps; but a remarkable old age pensioner, Mr Howard Morgan, who then lived nearby, remembered them. He had never worked at the Nurseries but knew Captain

Hill and remembered the tales he used to tell of the Chelsea Shows. As Mr. Morgan described the slug trap, it was baited with bran (a favourite with slugs) and as they ate it, they fell into the water at the bottom. It never failed, said Mr Morgan.

The catalogue itself had many illustrations, of which some were in colour. At first the coloured pictures were rather loosely stuck to a page, but later catalogues had full-colour pages, bound in, with brilliant hues.

1915 opened gloomily. The war, which was to have been over by Christmas, had accelerated. Those who tended the earth found that their occupation was more important than ever before; but gardeners enlisted as quickly as anybody, and the great gardens and gardening firms were soon seriously understaffed. Older men took the place of the young who had gone to fight, and women, trained and untrained, also played their part. The few Horticultural Training Centres for women ran special short courses. The slogan 'Dig for Victory' was a fairly early one, as the threat to the country's food supply became frighteningly evident.

Early in 1915 a remarkable exhibition of women's work was held at the Horticultural Hall, with agriculture and gardening well to the fore. The Lyceum Club, the first women's club to be established in London, organized a great part of this exhibition, and Dr Lilias Hamilton of Studley College gave an address. A conference was held at this time on the whole question of 'lady gardeners', with constant reference to the Chelsea Flower Show, posters advertising which hung in the Hall.

The Council of the RHS had given much thought as to whether or not the Show should go on. The RHS was faced with its own problems of declining membership, and though the real shortages of wartime had barely begun, there were always people to point out that decorative displays of flowers needed heat and extra labour – both of which should be diverted to the war effort instead.

However, the RHS realized (and has since abundantly been proved right) that had the many private and commercial cultivators abandoned their work, whole strains of beautiful plants would have been jeopardized, or even lost for ever. Later, of course, severe rationing of fuel and other commodities made cuts in gardens and nurseries inevitable, but dedicated gardeners struggled on none the less.

And in the meantime, largely as a result of the RHS's decision to continue with its fortnightly shows at Vincent Square as well as with the Chelsea Flower Show, horticultural societies up and down the country followed that lead, and carried on as best they could with local efforts. These country shows usually coupled their competitions with collecting vegetables and fruit for hospitals.

(In spite of hardships, some luxury plants continued to be produced. In 1915 smilax was still grown in quantities for table decoration. Even as staff dwindled and the country became enmeshed in war, it was inconceivable in large town or country houses, that dinner should be served without flowers and foliage trailing on a damask tablecloth, from the centre epergne to the place-settings. Those who have forgotten, or never saw this for themselves, may have been reminded or informed by ITV's serial, *Upstairs, Downstairs*.)

Criticism about the continuance of the Chelsea Flower Show came from within the Royal Hospital, too. Major-General C. J. Donald, closely in touch with Royal Hospital matters for many years (and a Commissioner of the Hospital as well) told my late husband that some of the pensioners were very indignant. He thought that it was probably because, being veterans and denied active service themselves, they resented seeing efforts by others directed to anything but the war.

However, the Show went on. Preparations were harder because of labour shortages. There were, of course, no big foreign exhibits, but messages of goodwill came from both France and Belgium, much of each country enemy-occupied.

The Show opened on 18 May 1915, and lasted for three days. Rain fell, and added to the sense of depression felt by most, for war news was bad that week, and the Show was smaller and had necessarily lost much of its glamour. Significantly, someone who attended remembers both flowers and people being more sober in colour, though this could clearly not have been true as regards the flowers. Roses, in fact, were brighter than ever, especially the new scarlet rambler of Messrs Paul of Waltham Cross. This lovely and hardy rose proved a godsend to many wartime gardens, for it seemed to thrive on a little neglect.

The *Gardener's Chronicle* writes of the Show:

'That there should be grumbling was but natural, but that there should have been so little is a tribute to the good nature and understanding of the visitors. It indicates that they are indeed gardeners, and recognized that the rain which inconvenienced them was doing good work elsewhere – in the country. In normal years the discomfort would have been reduced, but at the present time it proved impossible, owing to the scarcity of labour, to obtain a sufficiency of planks to bridge the seas of mud. Exhibitors also suffered in other ways; some of them found it impossible to persuade the railway companies to deliver their goods in time for staging, and others found that the inevitable curtailing of space pressed hardly on their exhibits. It is in these circumstances, however, that the British people are at their best, and it would seem almost as though they required the stimulus of adverse conditions to develop their serenest qualities. In spite of all, the great majority applauded the wisdom of the Society in holding the exhibition, and found in contemplating the wonderful exhibits some momentary relief and solace from the preoccupations of the war.'

An unusual collector for the War Horticultural Relief Fund was a very small Shetland pony, only three and a half feet high, led round the Show by the young Lord Dalrymple, dressed as a Colour Sergeant of the Scots Guards. The pony carried the collecting box, which was soon full. A special appeal which caught the imagination was for money to buy seeds later on, to replenish the devastated farm lands and gardens of Belgium and other countries, after the war. This was done, and seeds and plants were dispatched as soon as possible after the 1918 Armistice.

(Just before the invasion of the Low Countries in the Second World War, I spoke to a man who remembered this. I was in the Borrinage, mining country in Belgium near the French frontier, tracing the steps of people who had been connected with Edith Cavell. There I met an erstwhile British soldier called Tommy Colquhoun, who had stayed on after the war, married a Belgian, and who spoke of the help his family-by-marriage had received, and the gifts to replenish their little gardens.)

One touching war note at the 1915 Show was the enquiries made for friends not there. The main Enquiry Tent had some information – and often sad. There were also anxious queries about gardens and horticulture in occupied territories. Many people were referred to the *Gardener's Chronicle,* which published a weekly page in French of horticultural news from Belgium and France, with a short Flemish summary. This feature was ended in 1916, the reason given by M. van Oeshoven (an expert horticulturalist and regular enthusiastic attender at Chelsea shows) being that those refugees for whom it was intended were 'now so familiar with the English language as no longer to need to seek for news in their mother tongue'.

There was no band at the Show that year, for as someone commented, the soldiers were 'too busy elsewhere'. Civilian music had been suggested, but had been rejected as out of keeping with the Royal Hospital surroundings. Moreover, any financial saving was welcomed. The refreshment menu was written in plain English, rather than society French, though no reason for this was given. Advertisements in the catalogue tended to stress practicality and utility.

1916 saw the closing of W. Bull's Nurseries in the King's Road. Veitch's Nurseries had closed just before the war, so that Bull's was not only the last of Chelsea's great Nurseries, but almost the last of those in the metropolitan area. For years Bull's, which had its own Spring Show, had aimed at never clashing in date with that of the RHS, but at holding their show 'within reach', as an old employee put it, so that garden enthusiasts could use their absence from work to see both. Invitations to Bull's show, which had the added attraction of a fine conservatory, were issued, often verbally, at the Chelsea Shows of 1912 to 1915: Edward Bull, last of the family, always insisted that this was done, not so as to seek custom, but so as to share experiences. Besides, he would point out, in Bull's Nurseries there were plenty of seats and benches, which was not then the case at the Royal Hospital.

The report of the Annual General Meeting of the RHS, held in February 1916, announced that the Spring Show would be held in Chelsea on 23, 24 and 25 May, but that 'owing to the scarcity of labour, and other difficulties, the Council may have to forgo the Great Tent used in 1914 and 1915, and be content next year with a series of large marquees. . . .'

The Show opened in glorious sunshine – 'Hardy Flowers for Wartime' was its slogan. Vegetables and fruit were much in evidence, with 'toms and cues', as they were called, predominating. Mea Allen, in her book *Toms' Weeds* (Faber & Faber, 1971) about the famous house of Rochford (one of the most regular exhibitors at Chelsea and known world-wide for its house-plants), mentioned that the cucumber, which Pepys in 1663 had dismissed as 'fit only for the consumption of cows', was no longer considered a mere luxury for wafer-thin tea sandwiches, but was sent by the ton to coalfields and factories, as a useful refreshment in stifling atmospheres.

Despite the slogan, roses and orchids were on display in all their glory. A band played, patriotically selecting Elgar, Arthur Wood and Sullivan, and totally eschewing German music. Remarks were heard to the effect that music, like gardening, should transcend nationality, but it is thought that few regretted the omission of the tempestuous Wagner of 1914. Refreshments were adequate, but no more. The greatest change from previous years was the absence of the ever-popular rock gardens: a sad disappointment, necessitated by labour and transport difficulties.

The Show closed in driving rain, and was to be the last Chelsea Show till the war was over. But nearly all those who attended it returned a week or so later to the Royal Hospital for the great RHS Red Cross Sale, for which Owen Seaman wrote these lines:

Think not that Earth unheeding lies,
Tranced by the summer's golden air,
Indifferent under azure skies
What blows of War her children bear.

She that has felt our tears like rain,
And shared our wounds of body and soul,
Gives of her flowers to ease our pain,
Gives of her heart to make us whole.

4

The guns ceased firing at eleven a.m. on 11 November 1918. As discussions leading to the signing of the Peace Treaties dragged on, the weary nations came slowly back to an ordinary way of life, and people began to pick up the old pursuits which war years had forced them to drop.

Gardening in Britain had suffered less than might have been expected. Though research into all but essential plants and a few finer flowers had lessened or ceased, few of the big gardens, private or commercial, had closed completely. All, however, had cut down their activities, or were adapted to different uses. Production of fruit and vegetables was of first importance, for in 1919, and for some time afterwards, food was a major national problem. Flowers were grown partly for those leaves and petals used in medicine – some people will remember the collecting and drying of wild and cultivated foxgloves, which produce digitalis. Herb gardens were popular. But everybody in 1919 had to struggle with depleted man-power and difficult finances.

The RHS was swift to announce plans for the next Chelsea Show, though the year's Report stated:

> 'The decision having to be made so soon after the signing of the Armistice, it was far from certain, in those early days, what success it would be likely to meet with, and how far possibilities of tenting and labour, and indeed of exhibits also, would permit of the Show being held.'

Among the RHS's difficulties was that of administration, for their own Hall in Vincent Square had been requisition-ed by the War Office in 1917 for the use of the Australian Forces, and had not yet been returned to them. But the indomitable Secretary, the Rev W. Wilks, managed to circularize all the usual amateur and trade exhibitors, to find out whether they would be able to exhibit if a Chelsea Show could be arranged, and how much space they would need. Response was quick and good, but it remained to be seen whether tenting and equipment could be obtained.

It could. At the end of January 1919, the Rev W. Wilks confirmed to the Press that a show would be held in Chelsea in May, though it was decided early on to call it 'The Great Spring Meeting' of flowers, vegetables and garden sundries, and it was so described in advance notices and on the catalogue.

But a Show is a Show, whatever it may be called. The

RHS countered objections to holding such an event less than twelve months after the end of a war by stressing that the occasion was a practical one, with an emphasis on vegetables: and that the meeting would be partly educational, partly scientific, and partly to further the revival of the national pastime of gardening. The RHS also proposed that the meeting would be in aid of the Society's Wisley Garden Endowment Trust Fund, and the important practical and scientific work it had been set up to accomplish. (This fund, which fell within the definition of 'a charitable or philanthropic purpose', had been established in 1914.)

Most people were delighted at the thought of another Chelsea Show – it was something to look forward to in a country which, though at peace, was having anything but an easy time. There were still restrictions, rationing, and above all, there was grief and bewilderment at the terrible events of the last four bitter years.

The 1919 Spring Meeting opened on 26 May in glorious sunshine. All the famous flowers of the pre-war years reappeared, though displays were necessarily smaller. The sweet-pea, which had been threatened with complete disappearance in 1916, proved such forebodings false, and was shown in greater size and variety of delicate colours than ever. So also were violas and antirrhinums. Rock garden exhibitors met with difficulties as usual: 'some railway siding somewhere has the benefit of tubs and flagstones, rather than the slope towards the river at Chelsea', remarked one of them at the time. Tent accommodation was sufficient, in spite of anxieties, and in all, the Meeting Show fell only a little short of its splendid predecessors.

True to its word, the Council ensured that special consideration was given to vegetables and fruit. The displays of potatoes drew particularly large crowds, and recipes were handed out for its continued use as a substitute for other ingredients difficult to obtain. I remember learning to make a sponge cake with mashed potato instead of fine flour, from a recipe acquired at Chelsea in 1919.

Efforts were concentrated on making this first post-war show as educational as possible. Scientific lectures in the conference tent were well attended; there was information about allotments and small holdings, which had played a vital part in war years and whose importance extended into the years to follow. There were demonstrations on the uses of spraying, and at the Enquiry and Literature posts RHS booklets on jams and pickles were available alongside those of the four year-old Federation of Women's Institutes.

But the most prominent and interesting event, widely reported in the Press, was a conference on fruit-growing held under the joint auspices of the RHS and the Chamber of Horticulture. The Chairman, Mr George Munro, opened the proceedings with a call for more home-grown fruit. 'One of the biggest questions we have ahead of us in the future, in view of the financial state of the country as a result of the war, is to produce as much as possible ourselves and to import as little as possible.'

The principal speaker, Mr (later Sir) W. Lobjoit, emphasized the importance of good distribution, as he said the consumer is hardly benefited if 'the strawberries make lines of luscious scarlet on the fertile wealds of Kent . . . or if the plums bear down the laden limbs of the trees in Worcestershire and Middlesex, or the apple trees of Hereford and Cambridge make gold and scarlet landscapes, if means exist not for forging up the chain of contact between him and the produce itself.'

Mr Arthur Webb commented on a subject which has been discussed from time to time, until the present day. 'I think fruit growing should be encouraged on railway embankments. There are immense areas of land in England along the railway embankments. It may be news to some of you, but the Underground Railway are leasing certain small orchards to their employees for one shilling a year. I think they get sufficient land to grow twenty trees for two shillings a year. If the Underground Railway can do that, why cannot the great corporations like the Great Western Railway and the London and North-Eastern Railway?'

In these present days of economic difficulties, it is interesting to read of good intentions – many carried out, for a time – of over fifty years ago.

The *Gardener's Chronicle* adds a comment which throws light on the eating habits of those days, so recent and yet so different from ours. 'Those engaged in horticulture are apt to forget that the greater number of the inhabitants of Great Britain know little . . . of the value of fruit as a health food. . . . For the moment production cannot probably meet the demand, but in coming years it will be necessary to extend the home market by encouraging a large increase in the consumption of fruit.'

A press correspondent at the time remarked that it was difficult to find new adjectives to describe the yearly splendour of the Chelsea Shows. The same difficulty applies to me: once the personal memories and notes of the few remaining visitors to those early Shows have been given, it is hard not to descend to mere repetition year after year. So, while I shall mention new and exciting features, Shows from 1920 onwards must be less fully described.

The 1920 Show itself had variations on the former theme. It was held at a later date – the first three days in June. The tents, though not yet quite as large as before the war, were arranged so that one could pass between them without going outside. This should have been a great asset, but in fact proved the reverse. At some periods it was so insufferably hot that guests wilted along with the flowers.

For the first time in years, topiary exhibits reappeared. These, though not in themselves to everyone's taste, heralded the welcome possibility of once again concentrating on the purely decorative and time-consuming. One enthusiast expounded on the attractions of a pathway bounded by 'pyramids in Box . . . giving privacy in a large garden and appearing to give more space in a small one'.

However, a note of criticism sounded in 1920, from disgruntled gentlemen of the Press. The then President, Lord Lambourne, said that there were always grumblers, no matter what the Society did, and that the Society's duty was to show grumblers they were wrong. However, it appeared that the Press in this case had some cause – their facilities were inadequate, and some of them had been unable to obtain a press ticket until the very morning of the Show. There was also severe comment from the Trade on the parsimonious attitude of the Council to breakfast tickets for exhibitors' assistants.

The two following years, 1921 and 1922, brought the Shows back to their usual May dates. Grass gardens appeared among the Formal Garden exhibits, and in one there were stone figures which particularly caught the attention of King George and Queen Mary. This garden was exhibited by Messrs Macdonald and Sons, and one visitor commented that the stone seemed more at ease among the green grasses, than when it attempted to rival flowers.

In 1922 the Show's refreshment tents were moved into the Ranelagh Gardens, which gave them a feeling of leisured space, and in turn provided much-needed room elsewhere. The tent for educational and scientific exhibits was larger than before, and contained displays illustrating the experimental work done at the RHS garden laboratory at Wisley. An information bureau was staffed by RHS garden advisers and members of the Wisley staff, and was kept extremely busy answering all sorts of questions about gardening, as it always has been down the years.

The *Gardener's Chronicle* records 'An American's Impression of the Chelsea Show' after Chelsea that year – the visitor was John C. Wister.

'In recent years we have had many fine flower shows, but even the large size of our biggest national shows had left me unprepared for any show on such a gigantic scale as the 1922 Chelsea Exhibition . . . A group of plants that I admired particularly were the clematis hybrids exhibited by Messrs G. Jackman & Co, and one or two others. European gardeners are used to these, but to an American all but one or two varieties are totally new. I do not know how they would grow under our conditions. We are used to fine displays of roses in our American shows, and perhaps for this reason the roses did not impress me so much as some other flowers . . . I cannot close without mentioning how hungry I got every time I passed Laxton's wonderful strawberries, the like of which I have never seen. . . . '

One frequently recurring criticism of the Shows of the 1920s was that there were comparatively few new plants exhibited. The *Gardener's Chronicle* said that the object of such a Show should be to display to the world not only the present performance of British horticulture, but also its promise. Of the performance, it went on, no praise could be too high, but the increasing popularity of gardening meant there was a danger of the spectacular side of horticulture devouring the creative side, as the lean kine devoured the fat kine. With this Biblical analogy, the *Chronicle* rounded off its exhortation to British horticulture to continue with 'the improvement and discovery of new plants, and the encouragement of the cultivation of rare and difficult kinds of real garden value'.

More cheering at the time was the *Gardener's Magazine* of June 1922. 'The Chelsea Show yields the suggestion that after all the British Nation is still a going concern, and a rather sound one. There is no trace of decadence or despondency. There is enterprise and development.' And enterprise and development was badly needed, as the relief and security brought by the Armistice faded, and unemployment mounted grimly.

In 1923, Karel Capek's play, *Robots*, aroused intense interest. The word became part of the English language, and a lawn-mower was described as being 'Robot-like' on a stand at the 1924 Chelsea Show. Advertisements in the catalogues show how demands in gardening were changing – from the Exhibition in 1912 until the 1920s every catalogue had carried advertisements for 'horse boots', solidly-made leather overboots for a horse or pony pulling a mower, which avoided hoofmarks in well-kept turf. Mr G. N. Jaby, a senior member of the staff at Lord's Cricket Ground, confirms that horses were used until 1920 to pull the heavy roller, and were fitted with such boots. From the Twenties, however, mechanical mowers became increasingly popular.

The Torquay Wheelbarrow was another invention widely praised: its balance was such that it could easily be pushed on any gradient. The late Cyril Maude, famous actor, always used one on the steep slopes of his wonderful garden at Redlap, above Dartmouth; and later in Torquay itself.

The great 1924 Empire Exhibition at Wembley might have been expected to distract sightseers from Chelsea, but numbers were even greater, swelled by visitors to this country from all over the world.

In 1925, the Show was extended to five days. This meant that nearly all the plants shown were growing, as opposed to cut flowers, which could not last the week. There were still some great groups of cut flowers, however, and these often had to be renewed daily. Vegetables came in for extra comment this year. The famous Edwin Beckett, gardener at Aldenham to the Hon. Vicary Gibbs, really excelled himself, and his onions and root vegetables reached mammoth proportions. Challenged by a visitor, who claimed that their flavour must decrease with the increase in their girth, Beckett invited the lady in question to a friend's house in Chelsea, and himself cooked a mixture of his largest vegetables. No written record remains of the results, but it is understood that they proved as delicious as any tiny specimens.

The five-day Show was a success, but nevertheless it was decided to revert to three days in 1926. As it happened, the Show nearly failed to take place at all, as the miners' strike dragged on, and the General Strike threatened in the beginning of May. The RHS Report for that year says:

'The preparations for the Great Spring Show at Chelsea were attended by unprecedented difficulties. Owing to the General Strike, the contractors for the tents and the exhibitors of rock and formal gardens were greatly hindered in getting their material delivered, and in the end it became necessary to postpone the Show for a week. Fortunately weather conditions favoured a postponement, and when the exhibition opened it was unanimously declared to be equal, both in magnitude and quality, to anything previously seen at Chelsea.'

The Council passed a resolution on the first day of the Show (and circulated every exhibitor with a copy of it) thanking exhibitors for their efforts in spite of the most trying circumstances; for the attendance that year exceeded all records, despite curtailed railway services and the fact that the Show fell in Whit-week.

At the 1926 Show there was an extra tent for pictures of flowers and gardens – a suggestion that came from Her Majesty Queen Mary, whose knowledge of, and interest in, art was well-known. The late Mr William King, the great ceramic expert then at the Victoria and Albert Museum, wanted to show pieces of flower-decorated porcelain, which would have been appropriate with the site of the Chelsea China Works so near. A small committee of porcelain experts was formed early in 1926, but the plan came to nothing, because of the industrial disturbances. (Perhaps it may yet take place one year?)

The late 1920s saw a new feature linked to the Chelsea Shows, though not actually a part of them. These were the famous Chelsea tea-parties. Many people came up from the country for the Show, and many for just the one week of the year, so that people who lived near the Royal Hospital welcomed the opportunity of extending hospitality, as much as the visitors delighted in seeing their friends. (Though there was another, less kindly, way of putting it – 'A good opportunity to work off one's country acquaintances!')

It is possible that Lady Lovelace, who lived on Chelsea Embankment, and Mrs Hope-Nicholson, in Tite Street, were the instigators of this idea. However (or by whomever) it began, the custom flourished. In those earlier days, formal invitation cards would be sent, and some were even marked 'Please bring this card with you'. Tea near the Royal Hospital, after hours of flower-viewing – it sounded like a pleasant and refreshing rest, and indeed may have been so: but the effort involved in reaching the hospitable house often almost vitiated the rest awaiting. Even 'nearby' streets and squares are quite a long walk from the Show grounds, or (even in those days) were an expensive ride, always supposing there were anything available in which to ride. Taxis were scarce and private cars found it difficult to wait. Today, parking restrictions make it impossible.

But the tea-parties became an established custom, even in parts of Chelsea very hard to reach. The caterers at the Show were once asked if these parties took away much of their custom. Far from it, they replied: visitors often needed a good tea inside the grounds to fortify them for the journey to, say, Cadogan Square.

Those lucky enough to know the Governor of the Royal Hospital, or others on the staff, might be invited to tea there. Even then, unless met and escorted personally by their host, they would have to go out by the official exits, and walk round and in again at one of the main gates of the Hospital itself.

Whatever the difficulties of access, however, it was agreed that the Chelsea Flower Show tea-parties were delightful, and they were an acknowledged part of the London Season as it then was.

So the Twenties drew to a close, with much gaiety, but with depression on the way. In 1929 the BBC began experimental television programmes, the French began work on the Maginot Line, and the New York Stock Exchange collapsed. Depression loomed more threateningly still.

But at Chelsea, all was well. The 1929 Show saw exhibits almost doubled in number, and a dazzling display of primulas, which was the result of the Primula Conference of the previous year. A Mr A. Sherman Hoyt from Pasadena, California, produced the most amazing collection of cacti and desert plants ever seen in this country. Crowds gathered to stare at the strangely shaped, beautiful, succulent plants. Their children in later years were to know them well by sight: they were to come to typify Disney Land.

The third decade of this century began with severe industrial depression and ended in war. It saw the death of a beloved sovereign, the accession of two others, the abdication of one and the coronation of the other.

All these events were reflected in the horticultural world: flowers commemorated joy and grief; coronation trees, planted in 1937, were often chosen at the Chelsea Show. Among the influences on British gardening was the accession of a Queen with a great knowledge of the subject. The Lady Elizabeth Bowes-Lyon, as Queen Elizabeth had once been, learnt and practised gardening in the lovely grounds of her home, St Paul's Waldenbury, Hertfordshire. During her years as Consort to King George VI, she naturally had little free time for garden work, but her influence could be seen in all the Royal gardens. Those who had the honour to escort her round the Chelsea Shows know the extent of her real appreciation and knowledge.

1930 might be called Congress and Conference Year. An Imperial Botanical Conference was held in South Kensington; the Fifth International Botanic Congress was held in Cambridge; there was the Imperial Horticultural Conference at the Royal Society of Arts; and the Ninth International Horticultural Congress was ably organized by the RHS at Caxton Hall. Reports and papers

75

read at many of these conferences were obtainable at the 1930 Chelsea Show, which was held on 21, 22 and 23 May.

King George V had just recovered from a long, severe illness, so it was with special delight that he and Queen Mary were welcomed to the Show. They showed particular interest in a collective exhibit of fruit from the Dominions, in which the huge grapes from South Africa were outstandingly fine.

Among the judges that year was Mr Cyril Titchmarsh, who had had the difficult task, already mentioned, of marshalling exhibits for the 1912 Exhibition. More than fifteen years' experience since then had brought great changes. Another judge in 1930 was Miss Ellen Willmott, the great Rosarian, author of *Genus Rosa*. It was particularly appropriate that she should have been a judge, for 1930 was a 'roses year'. Never before, and rarely since, have they reached such heights of splendour. Many still recall Ellen Willmott, standing amid the glorious exhibits, saying she wished, like Alice in Wonderland, to give everyone a prize. With Miss Gertrude Jekyll, Miss Willmott was one of the two first women to be awarded the VMH – the Victoria Medal of Honour, chief award of the RHS. Her death four years later was a sad blow. 'She was a perennial,' someone commented.

Since the war, interest in herbs and salads had grown. Traditional recipes and cures for all manner of ills were discovered in Herbals and family 'Commonplace' books. Many such books were on view at Chelsea Show bookstands. One, which I particularly remember, was a collection of such recipes, with some original ideas added, by Marcel Boulestin and Jason Hill, published by

The nineteen-twenties: fashion and flowers outside the marquee

Laying out a water-garden
An all-too-familar scene at Chelsea

Summerhouses to suit all tastes

Fragile plants are gently staked

(Right) Crowds, with notebooks well in evidence, plan
purchases of lupins and delphiniums

Trophies and medals are the natural ambition of most exhibitors

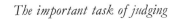

The important task of judging

A garden path between flower-beds inside the marquee

Queen Mary opens the Artists' tent in 1926

BACKEBERGIA
MILITARIS

PIPHY
LEME

SEDUM
PACHYPHYLLUM

Succulents (cacti) are more in evidence at each successive Show

An exhibit from Wisley Garden

The way to a perfect lawn

A woodland garden beneath the Royal Hospital trees

Heinemann in 1930. The seeds of Love-in-the-Mist (*Nigella damascena*) were recommended for their warm, aromatic flavour; and there was much emphasis on garlic, whose uses were less familiar then than now. It was once valued for keeping vampires away!

The weather that year was dull and cold, which was pleasanter for the flowers than the crowds. The big marquee was erected without its former division, which made circulation easier. The Sherwood Cup for the best exhibit in the Show was won by a superb display of vegetables from the gardens of the Hon. Vicary Gibbs. The redoubtable Edwin Beckett declared that this was the last time there would be such a display – a remark he often made, and which no one believed.

At noon on 22 May 1930, in the Show Conference Tent, a diploma was presented, under the common seal of the Society, to the first thirty Associates of Honour, elected by the RHS. With the diploma went a badge, which admitted the Associates free to any show, or other function, of the RHS. One Associate was Mr David Tannock, Superintendent of the Botanic Gardens in Dunedin, New Zealand: he was not himself present, but New Zealand was well represented by displays of fruit and flowers.

Outside the Show, there were a few demonstrators and people with placards proclaiming Hunger Marches and meetings. Unemployment figures were growing steadily. Though it was not widely known, the RHS, together with firms and private garden holders, employed as much casual labour as they could that year, both for preparation and maintenance of the Show. Much of the vegetables and fruit shown were sent on afterwards to the Occupational Centre for the Unemployed, in the crypt of nearby St Luke's, Chelsea.

1931 saw worse weather and financial conditions than its predecessor; and though at times the weather improved, the financial crises did not. The two great horticultural charities, the Gardeners' Royal Benevolent Institution and the Royal Gardeners' Orphan Fund, experienced no falling-off whatever in support and contributions, which was unusual in these hard-hit years when many charities found funds decreasing as their work and needs increased. Both horticultural charities are always represented at the Chelsea Shows, and more people called at their stands to enquire and contribute in 1931 and 1932, than ever before.

The show was held that year on 21, 22 and 23 May, with grey skies and real cold. The *Gardener's Chronicle* called it 'one of the best and one of the coldest'. The temperature on the day before opening, which is a critical day for final arrangements and judging, was coldest of all. Everyone suffered, including the Press: one journalist remarked that 'writing in a standing position, when it is so cold that the fingers can hardly control a pencil, is, to say the least of it, no fun'. However the Press, both national and horticultural, still managed descriptive and on the whole appreciative reports. The orchids were wonderful – 'never before have these aristocrats of the floral world been exhibited in such numbers and in such amazing variety'. There were fifty new species, which gained three First Class certificates and fifteen Awards of Merit. A group of orchids exhibited by Baron Schröder was described as being 'so fantastically beautiful that they could not be real . . . and one wasn't allowed to touch to see if they were'.

There were, surprisingly, no vegetable displays. Edwin Beckett had in fact spoken truly the year before: it had been his last exhibit. The fruit exhibits were few, but fine, with pot-grown trees of citrus fruits, plums, peaches and cherries from T. Rivers and Sons. Nearby, Messrs Laxton arranged their heavily-fruiting strawberries in half-moons, with baskets of picked fruit between them. There was also a memorable display of apples from G. Bunyard of Maidstone – more than sixty varieties, in silvered baskets against a blue background.

However, there were criticisms that year – and of the usually fulsomely praised model gardens, at that. Landscape architect Edward White said:

'I have taken part in judging the gardens at Chelsea Show almost continuously since the International Exhibition was held at Chelsea in the year 1912. This year I have not had the responsibility, and am free to state what I have been thinking for some time. Judging these gardens in any order of merit is a difficult and invidious task. The work of the judges would be much easier, and a desirable form of garden art would be encouraged, if in competitive entries *architecture* was invited to take a back seat.'

This comment was echoed later by landscape architect, R. V. Giffard Woolley:

'Some of the exhibits in this section appear to have "strayed" from the Sundries Avenue. There is, so far as one can see, no reason why large-scale models should not be shown there, using smaller plants (if possible of the same *genus*) to reproduce the effects of larger planting, but pigmy hard tennis-courts set in full-scale garden surroundings cannot be considered models'.

National and world-wide trade depression grew steadily worse, necessitating severe curtailment of public and private expenditure: yet 1932 could be described as one of continued horticultural progress. Tariffs on imported flowers, fruit and vegetables came into force in 1932, and this encouraged production of, and improvements in, home-grown varieties.

The death of the Hon. Vicary Gibbs, as well-known for his unique collection of shrubs as for the vegetables produced by his gardener Edwin Beckett, cast a gloom over the whole horticultural world, and beyond. As was said at the time, by a personal friend: 'He and Beckett have sown, the country reaps.' Many had learnt a great deal from the gardens at Aldenham and the displays at Chelsea, and in this difficult year of 1932, both private and trade vegetable growers had reason to emulate, and be thankful for, a great master gardener.

Leonard Sutton died too in 1932. His name had become, and remains, a household world to all who grow flowers and vegetables from seed. His presence, paternally supervising the magnificent Sutton Exhibits (often grouped round the monument), was sadly missed at Chelsea Shows.

The 1932 Chelsea Show saw an important innovation, which was not entirely successful. Fellows of the RHS were invited to a 'private view' from four p.m. to eight p.m., and hoped, by accepting this, to see the Show in greater comfort. One Fellow wrote: 'Those who possessed a sense of humour were amused at a "private view" attended by 15,000 or 16,000 people, but there were others who did not suffer patiently the long wait in car or cab entailed by the dislocation from Piccadilly to Pimlico. Whether the innovation is justified remains to be seen'.

Over forty years later, with changes made from time to time and some increase in space, the problem remains. Fellows' Day, or Private View, is as crowded as ever, and is likely to remain so, as the number of Fellows grows along with the fame and popularity of the Chelsea Show.

In 1931, organizers, judges and supporters had frozen: in 1932 they were soaked to the skin. Rain fell in torrents on the days before the opening. Water flooded the orchid tents, boxes floated to and fro, plants outside were flattened, and garden houses which were being exhibited were annexed as extra shelters. One of these fell to pieces. But the Show went on. Mud was its most prominent feature, but much use was made of duckboards and on the whole good humour prevailed.

In spite of the weather, it was a splendid occasion. Lilies predominated: begonias were slowly coming into their own; there were some delightful new climbing roses. Among the rhododendrons were specimens from Lionel de Rothschild at Exbury, which had been brought from the Mu Li mountains of China (where they grow at eleven thousand feet) and which had never before been shown.

After drenching the Chelsea Show, the weather in 1932 was to improve, with weeks of brilliant sunshine. The terrible unemployment figures began to fall, though only slightly: there was some little improvement too in the industrial and financial crises. But the World Economic Conference, opened that year in London by the King, had little success.

In co-operation with the directors of the Royal Botanic Gardens at Kew and at Edinburgh, the RHS staged the British section of another large flower show in Ghent. Flowers, fruit and plants came from private and public gardens. A Belgian remembers this exhibit well, particularly the demonstration by Messrs Sutton & Sons of how to make lawns and golf-courses – a truly British talent. Many names, familiar at Chelsea, appeared in the Ghent catalogue in April, to reappear a month later, with different exhibits, in the catalogue at Chelsea.

A sad death in 1932 was that of Lady Aberconway, VMH, mother of the Hon. H. D. Maclaren, who was then President of the RHS. A friend commented that she had left her own memorial in the shape of two beautiful gardens: one at Bodnant in Wales, and one at Château de la Garoupe, in France. Bodnant was, and still is, part of Britain's splendid horticultural history.

In 1933, the Show enjoyed fine weather, save for a downpour the first evening. After twenty years' experience, the organizers were now aware that rain should always be expected, and new drainage arrangements were being made, and improved yearly. In 1933 an enterprising exhibition among the Garden Sundries offered mackintosh hat covers and shoulder capes to visitors.

The carnations that year were magnificent, and Messrs

Allwood were presented with a First Class certificate for their deep scarlet carnation, *Robert Allwood*. Most of the rock gardens near the Embankment showed little variation, but one, from the Dartington Hall Garden Department, was exceptional. They had used local limestone and the deep red Devon clay to display rocks as though dragged from a wild coastline, above a stream bordered by primulas and other bright flowers.

Earlier in the year it had been forecast that electricity might soon supersede stove-heating methods in greenhouses. A trade paper commented: 'It is well within the bounds of possibility that there will be new developments, especially if electricity becomes available at a price to make its use a sound economic proposition'. There were already many signs of this change on various stands. Today electricity is in general use, though whether as a 'sound economic proposition' is open to doubt!

One practical exhibit, at another stand, was that of soil sterilization by electric power. This so fascinated a group of schoolboys from the north, that, though they were all sons of gardeners, they had to be forcibly moved from that stand to look at the flowers.

In 1934, which had a glorious spring and a long dry summer, the Chelsea Show opened later than usual, and lasted from 30 May until 1 June. HRH the Prince of Wales (later King Edward VIII) became a patron of the RHS that year, and was an early visitor to the Show, wandering about in his usual informal way. He had fairly recently bought Fort Belvedere at Sunninghill, with fine grounds: he wanted a rock garden, and quickly picked out a small but lovely one, which he ordered to be delivered in its entirety when the Show ended. A. J. Bull, Chelsea Contractors, the firm which worked at the Royal International Exhibition of 1912 and is still doing so today, undertook the job. The son-in-law of the late A. J. Bull remembers noticing a stranger among the workmen uprooting rocks and plants: enquiry revealed that the bare-armed, efficient worker was the Prince of Wales.

Other royal visitors that year were the King and Queen of Siam, who were shown the rhododendrons, and other species which originated in Asia. However, one of their escorts remembers them asking to see typical English flowers. Unfortunately, as the Show was held later than normally, tulips were less magnificent than usual, though there was a large and brightly coloured variety.

1935 was a joyous year, though very bad-tempered weatherwise. The Silver Jubilee celebrations for the accession of King George and Queen Mary were held early in May, and all London was a flower show. A cold spring with late frosts had not made it easy to set up and maintain the mountains of flowers and foliage, but park keepers, municipal gardeners, florists and private people managed to overcome the difficulties. Main streets and side streets (in some of which open-air tea-parties were later held) were filled with flowers: business frontages boasted ornate designs, private houses had simpler ones, with 'window gardens' rather than mere window-boxes. Where there was space for neither, bunches of flowers were placed in windows; or wreaths, as at Christmas, but made of spring flowers rather than holly, were hung on door knockers.

Jubilee Day, though windy, was clear-skied: the

Chelsea Show was not. May 22, 23 and 24 were bleak, with a cold northerly wind. Many exhibitors, by colour arrangements of red, white and blue, or by names for new plants, paid tribute to the Jubilee Year. A special Silver Jubilee Cup was presented by the RHS for the best exhibit by an amateur. Lionel de Rothschild of Exbury was a popular winner, for his rhododendron species and hybrids. His gardeners were Mr F. Hanger and Mr R. Findlay.

Mr C. Bartlett, then an under orchid-grower but today retired, helped stage this Jubilee Exhibit, and has written a vivid account of the infinite care taken in its preparation, which follows verbatim:

'I believe it was the first group of its kind and layout ever staged in this country. It caused a great deal of work at Exbury, the timing had to be exactly right, therefore a great number of staff were involved, even carpenters and sawmill staff. Mr Lionel supervised everything personally.

Everything was transported in the Estate lorries etc, involving trips night and day. (I do not think the late frosts played any part in this.) It was such that if plants reached Chelsea and were not to Mr Lionel's liking or standard when placed, back they had to come and more sent up, in fact it more or less meant that two groups were got up to choose from, till everything was perfect, and Mr Lionel won the Trophy. This group was a breakthrough in Show styles and set a style used very much to this day.

Alongside the Jubilee Group, orchids played a somewhat cagey part in it. We in the Orchid Department worked for months and held back some five to seven hundred plants of all *genera* in one big greenhouse, making a fantastic show, and the Horticultural fraternity and *us* were given to believe that Mr Lionel was going for the Trophy with orchids; then everything was switched and the concentration was on rhodes and azaleas.

Again Mr Lionel set up a standard which goes on today. He decided to put up a group of all Cymbidiums, most Exbury raised; a group of Cymbidiums was not a done thing in those days, and the orchid world were very sarcastic over it, but it was a very fine group which won him his usual Gold Medal.'

A well-known figure was mourned that year – Edwin Beckett, VMH, died in February 1935. Many tributes were paid him, including a very long obituary in *The Times*. His friends talked sadly of him during the Chelsea Show, at which for years he had played so distinguished a part. His knowledge and example lived on in the many young gardeners (including seven of his nephews) whom he had trained. A fellow-gardener, Fred Streeter, wrote of him: 'He was always ready to help those in distress. . . . As a judge, he was outstanding. . . . ' On his death forty years later, Fred Streeter himself was to receive still greater plaudits, not only from gardeners, but from the thousands who had listened to his warm voice giving advice on the radio.

A great sadness fell upon the whole country when King George V died on January 20 1936, at Sandringham, a home he and the Queen greatly loved, and in whose gardens they had made many improvements. Of his visits to the Chelsea Show, the *Gardener's Chronicle* wrote:

'He thoroughly enjoyed these visits, perhaps the more so because there was an absence of those formalities usually incidental to functions attended by Royalty. His Majesty, accompanied by his gracious Queen, did not merely walk round the great show, following a well defined route: he looked at everything, stopped to inspect exhibits that were especially interesting and attractive, asked questions of, and shook hands with, those in charge, paid personal compliments to those who won special honours, and frequently stepped back to draw Queen Mary's attention to some new or rare plant.

On one occasion, their Majesties short-circuited their escort and quite unexpectedly came upon the judges who were appraising the merits of the groups of orchids. Removing their hats, the judges stepped back to allow His Majesty to pass immediately in front of the groups then under consideration. Acknowledging their salute with a genial wave of the hand, the King said: "No, no! Please don't go away. I see you are judging, therefore you are much more important than I."'

The Chelsea Show of 1936 for once had good weather, neither too hot nor too cold. There were more exhibitors than the previous year, and much comment arose on the financial aspects of the Show. Expenses of exhibitors were immense, what with packing, transport, and arrangements, and all the labour that these involved:

and then there was the question of the value of the exhibits themselves. The orchids alone were worth enormous sums.

One group of these, shown by Messrs Black and Flory, was very distinctive in its arrangement. It was of Miltonias and Cattleyas, the larger Miltonias being displayed in the form of pyramids at either end of the main group, with the Cattleyas recessed in between.

1936 was the Silver Jubilee of the National Rose Society, and roses at the Show were excellent. They had a large tent to themselves, and were exquisitely and harmoniously displayed. The brilliantly coloured collection of Messrs Alex Dickson was especially noteworthy: the name of Wheatcroft, now so famous, was then coming to the fore, and in 1936 the firm concentrated on beds of dwarf Polyanthus roses.

The Sherwood Cup for the Show's most meritorious exhibit was won by Messrs H. Bolton and Son, for a beautiful display of sweet-peas. It was the first time these lovely flowers had been so 'decorated'. A much-applauded award was the Sutton Vegetable Cup, won by the Cheadle Mental Hospital (whose gardener was Mr C. E. Mason); much of the production work for the display had been done by the patients. This kind of therapy was in its infancy, but was later on to be widely and usefully developed.

Events at the end of 1936 are a matter of history. They resulted in a new King and Queen, George VI and Queen Elizabeth, both Fellows of the RHS, and both garden lovers. In honour of their coronation in 1937, the Chelsea Show that year staged a special feature. This was the superb Empire Exhibit, produced with the help of Kew

Gardens, and the Dominions and Colonies. Though some thought its appearance too sombre, with the dark heavy wood and foliage of many African plants and shrubs, it was nevertheless a splendid study of the diversity of plants within the Empire – on which in those days 'the sun never set'.

From Australia came many plants, including the famous gum trees and wattles (mimosa), some of them personally selected by HRH the Duke of Gloucester, then Governor-General of Australia. South Africa provided the centrepiece of the exhibit, with sweet-scented flowers; there were spruces and pines from Canada; great spreading tree-ferns from New Zealand, *Coffee arabica* from West Africa, brilliant gladioli from East Africa; and exotic flowers from India. The West Indies section, with its spice-bearing trees and bushes, was a blaze of colour and scent; Palestine contributed a very big, very prickly pear, and there were also exhibits from the Pacific Islands, the Seychelles, and even some little-known, sturdy plants from the Falkland Islands. A few of these specimens were borrowed from Kew, but nearly all the others travelled from their far homes for this great exhibit.

Elsewhere, there were very fine azaleas from Exbury, which won the Cain Cup – shown of course by Lionel de Rothschild, VMH, and his gardeners Mr Hanger and Mr Findlay. Messrs Allwoods' carnations, and their humbler relations, the garden (or Granny's) pinks, carried off the Sherwood Cup. A new Russell Lupin made its first appearance in a mixed collection of flowers, and was shortly to become immensely popular and easy to raise in London gardens. For some years, rock gardens on tabling had been exhibited: these were ideal for small alpine plants, and required much ingenuity. Though they could be set up out of doors, and were invaluable where space was limited, these small decorative gardens were also popular indoors.

At this time, flower arrangements for dining-tables and sitting-rooms had not become the subject of concentrated courses and study, as was to happen soon after the war. But in the mid-1930s, a new name appeared at RHS shows: that of Constance Spry, whose books, *Flower Decoration* and *Flowers In House and Garden* were published by J. M. Dent in 1934 and 1936 respectively. A keen member and admirer of the RHS, she had taken a small stand in the Sundries Avenue with some apprehension. At that time, as well as specializing in flower decoration, she was noted for beautiful but practical flower containers, in which white predominated; sheer white rooms and hangings were then much in fashion, though how these survived before the clean-air era is a mystery to housewives today. (And was a nightmare to housewives then, as I can confirm.)

Constance Spry's stand was a triumph of Flower Decoration, with large and exquisite arrangements. She was often asked at Chelsea, why there were not more groups of living-room size? Elizabeth Coxhead, in her biography of Constance Spry (William Luscombe, 1975) records that Mrs Spry grew weary of pointing out that such arrangements would be all but invisible to the Chelsea crowd. Her stand that year was to herald the new delight, craze, occupation – call it what you will – of flower arranging. But several years and another war were to pass before this came into its own.

Two deaths occurred in the Horticultural World just before, and just after, the 1937 Show. Mr William Hales died on 11 May – Curator of the Physic Garden from 1899 until his death, holder of the VMH and the Veitch Memorial Medal, a great pioneer in horticultural education. Sir Cecil Hanbury died on 10 June in the same year – it was to his father, Sir Thomas Hanbury, that the RHS owes the laboratory and garden at Wisley. Sir Cecil had figured in committee work and in active preparations for Chelsea Shows, of which he had rarely missed any. His family remembers how, though ill in 1937, he still studied the catalogue and made lists of the awards.

The weather, though never predictable, was particularly trying in 1938. A mild spring brought early fruit blossoms, which later cold blasts were to decimate. A hot dry period followed quickly on this cold spell, and plants flowered far too soon: many exhibitors had hastily to make new plans for the Chelsea Show. So excessively irregular was the weather, and so loud the complaints of trade and private gardeners, that the Press suggested the Chelsea Show might be abandoned.

But of course it was not; and it proved to be bigger, and almost more beautiful than usual. It was held in fair weather, on 25, 26 and 27 May. The Tuesday was now called 'Fellows Day', which many thought a better term than 'Private View'.

Rhododendrons were becoming yearly a more distinctive feature of the Show; a rhododendron congress had been proposed for the following year, but in view of the climatic difficulties it was decided to postpone it. One keen grower argued strongly against postponement, declaring that world affairs were even less certain than the weather. He was right. Though the Congress was announced at the Chelsea Show, to be held in 1940, it was in fact not held until 1949.

The Sherwood Cup was won that year by Messrs Blackmore and Langdon of Bath, with their dazzling, multi-coloured begonias, gloxinias and delphiniums. Colour was a dominant theme of the Show, for this year the RHS published the first volume of its *Horticultural Colour Chart*.

As choice of colour can make or mar an interior, so it is in a garden. Though colours which clash in fabric can mingle more freely in a flowerbed, care in choice can greatly improve a landscape, and for years this *Colour Chart* was to be the companion and guide of every dedicated gardener.

Tucked away in the fruit section were some pots of strawberries from Waterperry, the Horticultural School for women, founded and run by Miss Beaxtrix Havergal, VMH. It had opened in 1932, in the gentle Oxfordshire countryside, and these were the first of a series of triumphant medal-winning exhibits which were to follow after the war. Though Miss Havergal's school no longer exists as such, Waterperry is still connected with horticultural training. Miss Havergal herself lives in the grounds.

The advance notice of the 1939 Flower Show in the *Gardener's Chronicle* said: 'Moreover, should the weather keep fine, it is highly probable that there will be a record attendance . . . as thousands of people will be glad to forget the irritating and depressing influence of international affairs in the contemplation of beautiful plants and flowers, and attractive fruits and vegetables.'

The weather did not hold, there were gales and rain and cold; and world news worsened. Visitors passing the open spaces of London could see men drilling and digging trenches. However, one popular flower bene-fitted from the cold: tulips, often past their best by May, this year were resplendent. Messrs Barr and Sons' display won the Sherwood Cup, with acclamations from all. In the Scientific Section, an exhibit which attracted much attention was that of the John Innes Horticultural Institute, showing the growing of seedlings in a special compost. An association called Men of the Trees demon-strated tree-planting to large crowds.

But there was, as always, some criticism. A letter in a horticultural journal, headed 'Monotony at Flower Shows', decried the 'colossal' exhibits year after year, and the sameness of arrangements. It ended: 'The worst advertisement a Show can have, is when visitors say it is exactly the same as last year.'

But after 1939 there was to be a pause of eight years, and for better or for worse, nothing was ever to be exactly the same again.

The Second World War ended in 1945, but the years that followed were far from peaceful, and adjustments once again had to be made to the way of life that followed so long a period of hostilities. Like many organizations at that time, the RHS had severe problems. Costs of wages, fuel and postage had soared, and so subscriptions rose too, though this was resisted by some. It is a tribute to both the organization and its members, that in 1945 the total membership fell only by 271; and by 1950 the numbers had risen to 38,268, passing the pre-war total by 2,000.

With more subscription money coming in, it was hoped that the Society's activities could begin again and pay for themselves. But when the President, Lord Aberconway, proposed the revival of the Chelsea Show, he met with fierce opposition. Still, he said firmly in October 1946: 'Whatever else we go without, we should not go without a Chelsea Show next year', and so it was planned for 21 May 1947.

There were many difficulties to be overcome. The First World War had seen the suspension of the Show for only two years, but the Second had meant a gap of eight. Demand for food production during the war years had led to drastic changes at nurseries: greenhouse plants were in very short supply. Transport costs looked like making large exhibits and rock gardens almost impossible. But the President and his supporters stood firm, and the Show opened on schedule.

The Show was about two-thirds the size of the last one, in 1939, and had fewer surprises – except for its being there at all. But nevertheless it was splendid and hopeful, and deserved its headline in the *Gardener's Chronicle* of 31 May 1947 – 'A Horticultural Renaissance'.

It was a time for happy reunion among friends who had not met since before the war – though changes were apparent. One woman Fellow remembers hesitating as a friend of pre-war days approached her, and seeing a reciprocal expression of uncertainty, even of horror, on her friend's face at the alterations wrought by the war. But if people changed, the flowers did not, though some were differently displayed. Since there were fewer orchids, these were distributed round the tents, and not exhibited together as usual.

The Gold Medal that year went to a magnificent display of rhododendrons in full bloom, from Bodnant, Wales, home of Lord Aberconway. His gardener, Mr Puddle, said that the difficulties of the long journey had been terrible; and there was general delight at the award, not least because it was Lord Aberconway's persistence which had resulted in there being a Show at all. Among the joys of the Show was that of seeing again an abundance of colour after the drab war years, and it was held to be a matter for congratulation that the RHS had, in the difficult year of 1942, managed to produce a second volume of the *Horticultural Colour Chart*.

1948 saw the Chelsea Show looking almost as it had done before the war, though with some innovations. The Women's Voluntary Service (now the WRVS) showed a garden suitable for the pre-fabs which were springing up everywhere in an attempt to solve the terrible housing shortage. Little flower-beds bright with salvia and nemesias were displayed in the front garden, with vegetable plots behind. This exhibit was part of the London Gardens Gift Scheme, designed to help those returning to war-damaged houses to 'make the rubble blossom'. Until 1955, it was a yearly event, and it won both Flora and Banksian silver-gilt medals for the WVS. At the WVS stands, the public was requested to donate seeds, plants and gardening equipment, and there was a generous response.

Before the 1948 Chelsea Show opened, the *Gardener's Chronicle* had carried a brief announcement of a new event – 'In conjunction with the Show there will be two Flower Arrangement Competitions, one for professional horticulturalists, and the other for amateurs'. So began a regular event which to some has become the most important feature of Chelsea Shows, while others consider it should not be there at all. Many gardeners felt then, and journalists pointed out, that while flower arranging was an admirable art, it had really no right to precious space at Chelsea; and to this day there are those who think the cult has grown out of all proportion, and that however much happiness and beauty it brings into lives and homes, the Chelsea Show is not the place for such competitions.

It is not easy to decide when the act of placing flowers and foliage in containers for house and table decoration ceased to be merely a pleasant extension of flower-growing, and became a 'Movement'. But a movement it now is. Organized in this country round a central body, the National Association of Flower Arrangement Societies of Great Britain, to which smaller clubs can be affiliated, there are at present more than 100,000 people of both sexes, all ages and occupations, and from every section of the community, who belong to Flower Clubs and Societies.

Though flower arrangement as an art has been practised for centuries, it began to be a serious study in this country just before the Second World War, and owed much to Constance Spry. This unusual woman, who died in 1960, had prodigious talents. Her work as a professional florist, in which capacity she first exhibited at Chelsea, gradually extended to training others and to writing about flowers, as well as growing them. Her name is world-famous, and the yearly displays at Chelsea by the firm which bears her name are a joy to behold.

In 1947 two very remarkable women were laying foundations for what was to prove such pleasure and interest to many. Julia Clements (later Lady Seton, who received the VMH in 1974 and is also a well-known writer on flowers and their arrangement) went to America for a lecture tour. She travelled in the same ship as Lord Aberconway, President of the RHS, who was to be Guest of Honour at the International Flower Show in New York. Julia, in her lectures, described the important part gardens and gardening had played in the war years, as regards morale as well as practical use. When she returned, she was determined to form flower arrangement clubs to help combat post-war austerities and depression.

Meanwhile in Dorset Mrs Mary Pope was active in forming the first Flower Arrangement Clubs. The two women – Julia town-based in Chelsea, Mary country-based in Dorset – were the pioneers of what has grown into one of the most remarkable movements in Great Britain. One has only to see the queues which form for the Flower Arrangement Tent at the Chelsea Show (where both Julia Clements and Mary Pope are leading judges) to realize how interest in the subject has swept the country, and that, whatever the critics may say or write, Flower Arrangement is now an ineradicable part of the Show.

In 1948 there were fewer individual fruit and vegetable exhibits than previously, but the stand of the National Farmer's Union made up for this with a remarkable arrangement composed of flowers, fruit and vegetables, designed by Violet Stevenson, well-known author and journalist, in conjunction with Mr E. R. Janes of Sutton's. An exquisite floral display, of pinks against a silver background, was the creation of Pamela Underwood, a renowned horticulturalist from Colchester, who earned herself the charming nickname, 'The Silver Lady', from the silver-leaved plants in which she specializes.

There was another important change in 1948 – the Mayor of Chelsea was invited in his official capacity for the first time, as he or she has been ever since. It took a good deal of correspondence between the RHS and the Borough of Chelsea to ensure this. As has been explained in an earlier chapter, the Governor of the Royal Hospital takes precedence over the Mayor on the Royal Hospital grounds, but in 1948, for the first time, the then Mayor of Chelsea, Alderman George Tonbridge, stood with the President of the RHS to receive the Royal party.

The Chelsea Show had regained its pre-war excellence by 1949. It now covered about eleven and a half acres, of which nearly three acres were under canvas: even then, exhibitors had to be turned away. In this year, the Private View or Fellows' Day was reinstated, and has continued ever since.

The Lawrence Medal that year was won for the first time by the Crown Estate Commissioners, for a woodland garden with primulas growing beneath rhododendrons, azaleas and other bright-leaved shrubs. Those who today delight in Windsor Great Park's Savill Garden, which inspired this entry, are seeing the brain-child of a great man – Eric Savill, later to become Sir Eric. When he was appointed Deputy Surveyor of Windsor Parks and Woods, there was then no garden in the Park at all, and in 1932 he chose a woodland site, and began to transform it. A great many plants were gifts from his friends (including Lord Aberconway and other Council members of the RHS), and descendants of these plants can be seen there today.

There was only one exhibit from the Continent – M Vanderlinden's azaleas from Belgium. Together with rhododendrons, these lovely flowers were becoming an increasingly noticeable feature of the Chelsea Shows. The Rhododendron Conference planned for 1939 took place a month before the 1949 Chelsea Show, and a Camellia Conference was planned for 1950.

Horticulturally, the 1950s began full of hope. If war years had given a boost to the growing of fruit and vegetables, peace time encouraged the pleasures of flower-gardening – and from the attendance at conferences and the crowds round the Chelsea Show enquiry stands, it seemed that every kind of gardener was eager to learn. 1950 was Quinquennial Year for the 'Floralies' at Ghent – the first since before the war – and the dazzling splendour of such a show, in a country that had been so completely enemy-occupied, was an inspiration and encouragement.

The Chelsea Show of 1950 had both sunshine and rain: the roads of the Royal Hospital had been tarred and the drainage improved, which meant less of a morass when the storm broke. In 1941, Edward Sweetings had been appointed Superintendent of the grounds of the Royal Hospital, and many innovations and improvements were due to him.

At the Press luncheon that year, Lord Aberconway dealt pointedly with the perennial complaints that the Show grounds were overcrowded: no one, he said, expected to have the Derby or a Test Match to himself, so why the Chelsea Flower Show?

If crowds caused complaint every year, there was real reason for concern in 1951. This was Festival Year, and many visitors to the festivities timed their trip to

London to take in the Flower Show as well. Luckily there was an immense new marquee that year, covering three and a half acres – the largest ever erected in this country. This was still the handiwork of Messrs Piggott, who had made what had then seemed the 'outsize' marquees of the first shows at Chelsea, from 1913 onwards.

In 1951, Mr A. Simmonds succeeded Brigadier C. V. L. Lycett as Secretary of the RHS. He had long been Deputy Secretary, and in fact spent his entire career with the RHS, beginning as a gardener trainee at Wisley in 1907 (together with Mr Cartwright and Mr Titchmarsh). He had been concerned with Chelsea Shows since their beginning. To this day his name is remembered with affection, especially by the older workmen preparing the site. He retired in 1962 and died in 1968.

The country was plunged into real sorrow when, early on a February morning in 1952, it was known that King George VI had died; but the welcome given to the new young Queen was possibly warmer than any recent monarch had received. And the close ties the Royal Family has always had with the gardening world strengthened as the years went on.

May 21 to 23 was the date of the Show in 1952, and it was a wonderful one – if this must be said again, it is true, and not idle repetition. The previous year's successful experiment of erecting one huge marquee was repeated: there it was, and it needed an effort of memory to believe it had ever been otherwise.

The first Spanish garden to be shown at Chelsea was a great feature. The Sociedad de Amigos del Paisaje y Jardines de Madrid sponsored the display, which in addition to Spanish plants featured the grilles and gates in ornate ironwork typical of the country. The main construction work was done by Messrs William Wood and Sons Ltd, one of whose employees at the time confessed that it was difficult to follow the voluble instructions of the Spanish experts supervising the final touches.

The Spanish garden showed the kind of vistas and ideas which were hard to achieve in this country and climate; but the most important features of the rest of the Show were the exact opposite. Emphasis was on easier gardens at lower cost, and from 1952 the gardens shown came steadily nearer the reach of every pocket, without lowering horticultural standards.

1953 was Coronation Year, and came in with weather that was appallingly inclement, even for a decade which seemed to produce little else. The Chelsea Show, however, shone as brightly as usual; though as its date was barely a week before the Coronation itself, Her Majesty the Queen naturally could not attend. Many of the Royal Family were there, however, along with even bigger crowds than usual, as people flocked to London for the Coronation celebrations. A Commonwealth Exhibit, staged by the Royal Botanic Gardens at Kew, was reminiscent of earlier Empire displays – except that among the exotic and strange plants from overseas was a simple woodland glade made up of very British shrubs.

There was sadness that year as well as rejoicing, with the death of Her Majesty Queen Mary. Her love of flowers and trees, like her knowledge and love of antiques, had inspired professionals and amateurs alike. She had hardly ever missed a Chelsea Flower Show, sometimes returning on a private visit to see again those plants she had especially admired. As patron of the National Rose Society, she would often pick out some variety at Chelsea, criticizing as well as praising. Among her special loves were delphiniums (she had arranged striking borders of these at Sandringham); among her dislikes was ivy, which she saw as a menace to old buildings, and to which she objected even as a decorative addition in flower arrangements. The rose beds in Queen Mary's Garden in Regent's Park remain perhaps her greatest memorial, but as well as grand formal gardens, she also interested herself in the window-boxes and back gardens of the smaller streets.

There were other losses to the gardening world in 1953. One was that of Thomas Hay, CVO, VMH, who died in January. His superb work as Superintendent of the Central Royal Parks remains today, in the shape of plants and trees well chosen and skilfully arranged. It was a source of real grief to him that a rare treasure, the *Daphne sophia*, which had been first brought to this country in 1939 and had flowered the year after, had been destroyed by enemy action in 1941.

The RHS itself lost a remarkable President, Lord Aberconway. Dr H. R. Fletcher wrote of him: 'Possessed of extraordinary initiative and drive, he eschewed delay in reaching decisions or hesitation in giving effect to them . . . all his life he had been a truly great gardener. Not content to collect and grow choice plants, he desired if possible to improve them and thus devoted much time, knowledge and skill to hybridization.' In twenty years, forty-four hybrid rhododendrons received Awards of Merit from his renowned garden at Bodnant, and fifteen the First Class certificate.

The Hon. (later Sir) David Bowes-Lyon succeeded Lord Aberconway as president of the RHS. It was a welcome appointment, and it was generally considered that he was probably the only man who could have followed immediately and effectively in the footsteps of his illustrious predecessor. Two months later he presided at the great dinner to celebrate the RHS's Sesquicentenary – a dinner which was notable for the number of women who attended, not only because they were Fellows, but because they were renowned in the horticultural world.

1954 marked the Sesquicentenary of the RHS. One distinguished nurseryman had thought to choose some special plant and name it after this great anniversary – but in the event he decided the pronunciation was difficult and the sound not very harmonious, however important the occasion.

The shows of 1954 and 1955 were considered slightly disappointing by some. As usual the weather, in the words of a West Country gardener, 'could be relied upon to be unreliable'. A warmly welcomed visitor in May 1954 was the Duke of Windsor, who ordered many plants for the garden he was making at his Millstream home in France. There were more vegetable exhibits than usual, especially early varieties. At this period, frozen vegetables were gaining in popularity in the shops, and one exhibitor in 1955 saw these as a serious competition to early vegetables and such seasonal delicacies. However, no one yielded in the struggle, and one vegetable exhibitor that year handed out easy instructions for home-grown *primeurs* – a French term for early peas, carrots and the like, which does not translate readily.

1956 saw the Chelsea Show its radiant self again (though few had noticed that it had ever been otherwise). Allwoods' carnations won the Gold Medal yet once more, and the Wisley Garden rhododendrons were more spectacular than ever. One of these, *Yakushimanum*, had been introduced from Japan just before the war, and already fifty crosses had been made from it at Wisley. Some of these hybrids were quick-flowering, beautiful and hardy, and they attracted a great deal of interest and many orders.

This was the first year that the Minister of Agriculture (the Rt Hon. D. Heathcote Amory) attended the luncheon given for Press and Committee members, though previous Ministers had visited the Show in their private capacity. It was also the first year in which the Flower Arrangement Societies had a marquee to themselves, as they have had ever since. One exhibitor that year said that it felt like being besieged in the tent, so large and insistent were the crowds outside.

In 1956 Mr R. Sargent took charge of the Show's office at Vincent Square, where he still is. He had been in that office since 1934, having joined the RHS in 1929. His chief assistant is his wife.

The Chelsea Show has always been a happy place for encounters. Some faces, those of officials, exhibitors or even visitors, become so familiar year after year that they seem almost old friends. The *Gardener's Chronicle* of 18 May 1957 published two pages of photographs of leading exhibitors, with their comments on what they were preparing for the coming Show. These were such well-known gardening names as Mr Montagu C. Allwood, Mr D. A. Baker, Mr J. H. Bolton, Mr W. H. Dunnett,

Mr John W. Fife, Mr H. G. Hillier, Mr F. P. Knight, Mr Allan Langdon, Mr D. Noel Sutton, Mr Harry Wheatcroft and Mr Harold G. Whitelegg. Visitors were seen at the Show with these pages in hand, looking for the real-life subjects of the photographs. One exhibitor said, 'Harry Wheatcroft can easily be recognized, his moustaches are as well grown as his roses.'

One group of visitors that year attracted special attention. These were eight pensioner-gardeners, from the Royal Gardeners' Benevolent Institution then near Slough. Fisons Limited had organized transport to and from the Show, with refreshments as well. Members of the firm took them slowly round the whole Show, three in bath chairs. What seemed so extraordinary was that only one of them had ever been to a Chelsea Show before – nearly forty years previously.

The *Gardener's Chronicle* commented: 'Of course, Chelsea comes just at the time when a gardener has much to attend to, but it came as a surprise to us that at no time in their gardening life had seven of these old gardeners been sent to the Chelsea Show by their employers. We would think that attendance at a Chelsea Show now and then should be almost a compulsory duty for every gardener.'

This absence from Chelsea was in no way typical of the gardener/employer relationship. From the earliest years, employers would travel to Chelsea with their gardeners and together they would cover the whole Show – the gardener generally a step or so behind with the notebook. There was one tall, elderly lady, her hat almost outdoing the exhibits, her sturdy but also ageing gardener carrying an enormous magnifying glass. The gardener examined the flowers carefully with this glass, ceremoniously holding it for her when she wished to see, or write an order.

1958 was a year which I vividly remember. My late husband was then Mayor of Chelsea, and it was a fascinating experience to visit the Show as a guest of honour. Among the sights of special interest I remember was the arrival of the Royal Family on the Monday afternoon.

The reception party was drawn up in a line leading to the Embankment entrance, where members of the Royal Family arrive at ten-minute intervals. They begin with the most junior members (that year it was Princess Alexandra, some time before her marriage) and end with the Queen. Each is received by a member of the Council of the RHS, together with a leading Nurseryman or Seed Merchant; the Council members stand in order of seniority, with the President at the end of the line farthest from the entrance, waiting to receive and show round the Queen. It might be tactless to enquire how precedence is settled on for their companions, but in 1958, the President, David Bowes-Lyon, had a member of the Sutton firm beside him.

This was the year of the wonderful French *Potager*, exhibited by Vilmorin-Andrieux and designed by an Englishman, Russell Page. Roy Hay described this in an article in *The Times* in 1975:

'Some fifteen years ago, my friend André de Vilmorin . . . said he would like to stage an exhibit at the Chelsea Flower Show, but he wanted it to be something unique, something we had never seen at Chelsea. . . .

I suggested that he create a typically French *jardin potager*, with the fruit trees trained in all the different shapes . . . as low espaliers round beds of flowers and vegetables. . . .

You want to ruin the firm, he said.'

But this superb *potager* was duly set up, with flowers under the apple trees near neat rows of leeks and lettuces. It won a Gold Medal and became the admiration and talking point of the 1958 Show. Some of the beautiful trees were left behind as a present, and planted in the Ranelagh Gardens. 1958 was also the first year the BBC Television mounted a full-scale coverage of the Show – though not yet in colour.

1959, the last year of a decade that some were glad to see ending, provided for once a real heat-wave in May. The Show was later than usual (26–29 May) and so the exhibitors had some difficulty in 'timing' the show blooms. But as has often been said, no weather can be right for every gardener all the time, and Chelsea offers just one example of how man can triumph over circumstances. The Press had a special place at this year's Show, for *The Times* had an exhibit – The Garden of Tomorrow – designed in conjunction with the *Gardener's Chronicle*, and constructed by George C. Whitelegg. It was ingenious as well as decorative, and heralded the age of technology by showing a radio-controlled lawn-mower at work on its own. One newspaper artist, gloomily watching it charge along, said that if there was one of these in every home, an extremely profitable subject for cartoons would be gone forever.

The Royal Botanic Gardens at Kew showed an

amazing collection of tropical plants, including cotton in fruit and flower, as well as breadfruit, rice and bananas. It seemed fitting that they should be shown at Chelsea, for less than a quarter of a mile away is the Chelsea Physic Garden, where Dr Nathaniel Ward invented the Wardian Case which made it possible for seeds and plants to travel from one climate to another without deteriorating on the long sea voyages. Without that case, and without the plant-collecting voyages of Robert Fortune which were backed by the RHS, many plants in the Kew Exhibit might never have reached this country. Nor might it have been so easy to seek a 'cuppa' in the Refreshment Tent: for between 1848 and 1852, Robert Fortune, on behalf of the East India Company and complete with Wardian Case, made several journeys from China, taking tea to be cultivated in Assam.

The new decade came in with the promise of exciting horticultural events. 1960 was heralded as Orchid Year, and rightly so, for the Third World Orchid Conference took place in London from 20 May to 2 June. The Chelsea Show that year fell within this period, 25–27 May, thus doubling delights for orchid-lovers. H. R. Fletcher writes that 'the orchid enthusiasts made Chelsea a very invigorating and somewhat light-hearted affair'.

The fabulous beauty of orchids on a corsage, in a hothouse or gloriously banked in the Flower Show marquee, typifies wealth and fashion. A history of peril, sacrifice, money and passionate determination lies behind their discovery in exotic parts of the world, and their transference to, and cultivation in, Britain. But it is well to remember that Britain has its own orchid, the tiny wild plant which grows in meadows around this country. Luckily it hides itself well, for, like much else, this exquisite little bloom is threatened by vandals, bulldozers and pollution.

One summer there was a Flower Show at the West Country house where Tennyson once lived, and wrote *Come Into the Garden, Maud*. A small girl who entered for a wild flower competition earned herself a prize of 6d, and a stern rebuke from Miss Bella Lister, one of the judges and a fine botanist of the famous scientific family. The child's winning bunch contained a Bee Orchid. David Sander (whose name and displays are well known at Chelsea) writes in his book *Orchids and Their Cultivation* (Blandford Press, 1969): 'I have once in my life seen this orchid wild, in an area which I dare not mention for it [the flower] is now so rare.' May Britain's orchids thrive in safety!

Names of famous orchid-growers echo down the years, and include commercial nurseries, Research Stations, individuals and Botanic Gardens, as well as such famous families as Rothschild, Schröder, Colman, Veitch, Charlesworth, McBean, Sander, Holford, Black and Flory. This list could also include the superb craftsmen-gardeners who worked with the private and professional people. Two of these must be mentioned as having special relationships with Chelsea.

H. G. Alexander, who died in 1972 aged ninety-seven, was awarded the VMH in 1926, and was orchid-grower to Sir George Holford at Westonbirt. In 1960 Mr Alexander provided the money which funds the gold Westonbirt

Orchid Medal, for cultivation and other outstanding achievements related to orchids.

Mr B. F. Perfect was orchid-grower to the late Sir Jeremiah Colman, and it was generally agreed that the name typified the man. Superb *Lycaste Skinneri* cultivated by him at Gatton Park, won awards at many a Chelsea Show. It is an orchid which has many links with Chelsea, though it originated in Guatemala. The very first Lindley Medal was gained in 1865 by Messrs Veitch of King's Road, for more than fifty specimens of the lovely blooms.

It is not generally known that Vanilla, whose seed-pods are used in cooking, is an orchid too. The great Maître-Chef, Escoffier, always hoped to grow his own pods, but never succeeded.

1961 and 1962 saw a forecast of things to come at Chelsea. Though the Science exhibits in both years took up less space, they were of intense importance, with many original ideas. The Bee Research Association, which always mounted an impressive display, had models showing the process of pollination as well as more illustration charts and leaflets than ever, to inform the ignorant – and even occasionally the expert. Posters appealed to private citizens and local authorities to provide forage plants for bees, especially in the New Towns. It is interesting to note that not far from the Royal Hospital is a flourishing hive of bees – one reason perhaps why Chelsea as a borough has such a wealth of flowers.

There was a general emphasis on insect life in those years. East Malling Research Station dealt with the development of beneficial insects, while Wye College (University of London) concentrated on the harmful ones – including that horrific small creature, the black-currant sawfly, *Pteronida olfactens*. This tiny insect had only been identified about twelve years previously, by which time it had done a great deal of damage. Rothamsted Experimental Station worked on enemies of the potato; the Glasshouse Crops Research Institute on enemies of the tomato. Experiments were constantly being made with insecticides, to see which were effective with which insects.

The argument mentioned earlier, about whether Britain should have a longer, bigger, more spectacular Flower Festival than a three-day show at Chelsea, began again in 1960, probably because it was a year of splendid flower shows abroad. There was the Quinquennial 'Floralies' at Ghent, where Great Britain was admirably represented – decoratively with wood and water gardens, scientifically with a greenhouse incorporating every modern device of heating and ventilation; and there was also the 'Floriade' in Rotterdam, where the Royal Botanic Gardens at Kew had a superb display, authorized by the Queen.

So many enthusiasts asked: 'Why not here?'

The Chelsea Flower Show is a beautiful market-place frequented by garden-lovers: the 'Floralies', and its equivalents in Europe and the USA, are primarily spectacles which present horticultural products to a lay public with very little gardening knowledge. More than just money would be needed for Britain to produce a show on this scale – perhaps space would be the greatest problem of all. Sir David Bowes-Lyon, President of the RHS, said the following year that Chelsea 'is bursting at the seams, with not nearly enough room for us to do as we would like'. The *Gardener's Chronicle*, at the time of the discussion in 1960, said: 'Britain is not an important horticultural exporting nation, though we are perhaps the greatest nation of gardeners in the world.' At any event, though the matter was widely argued at the time – and indeed has been argued regularly since then – no action has yet been taken.

In September 1961, the RHS suffered another sad loss in the death of its President [Sir David Bowes-Lyon.] His eight years of Presidency had included the Sesquicentenary, the World Orchid and other major Conferences, and many brilliant Chelsea Shows. To all of these Sir David had given great attention to detail, and his appreciation of the efforts made to ensure success. Those privileged to walk round the Show with him knew that he added to his many qualities a sense of fun. Eight years is not long, but the results of his inspired Presidency still continue.

His death left a vacancy among holders of the VMH, of which there are only sixty-three. (When it was instituted in 1897, there were only sixty – a number chosen to mark the years of Queen Victoria's reign at the time. When she died, however, a further three were added.) When it was known that this vacancy would be filled by the gracious acceptance of Her Majesty, Queen Elizabeth the Queen Mother, there was public acclaim. It was the first time that a brother and sister had both been awarded the VMH.

Lord Aberconway succeeded as President, a post he holds with much distinction to this day. He holds it by right of his knowledge and achievement, but the feeling that it was a 'family' accession delighted many. Lord Aberconway represented the third generation of his family to hold the VMH, which his father (a former President of the RHS) had received in 1934, and his grandmother in 1931.

Also in the autumn of 1961 came news of the death of the Curator of Wisley, Francis Hanger. He had been Curator since 1946, and had been largely responsible for the many magnificent Wisley exhibits at Chelsea since then. However, the inspiration and the splendid staff he left behind him ensured that these would continue.

Horticultural progress and change continued to be recorded at Chelsea. Will Ingwersen, writer and gardener, commented: 'Much as I love stately delphiniums, I hate tall stakes to hold them up, so they are taboo in my windswept garden. This made me rejoice to see "Blue Tomtit", whose three to four feet sturdy stems will surely stand without support, and whose well-filled spikes of deep violet-blue are just as lovely as its taller cousins.'

A fine feature that had begun earlier, but which reached its zenith in the 1960s, was the Waterperry strawberry exhibit, to which reference has been made in Chapter 4. Miss Beatrix Havergal, who received the VMH in 1965, was already famous for her horticultural school for girls (at Waterperry in Oxfordshire), for her downright character, and for the strawberries which appeared year after year at Chelsea. They always gained a medal, and this was almost always a Gold. She was a keen observer and kept a diary each year from early April until the day the strawberries left the nursery for Chelsea. Here is an extract from an early diary:

The Queen Mother enjoys a strawberry

A pensioner at the Show
The Constance Spry Stand 1954

A gold medal for vegetables
Roses: a 1973 exhibit

Her Majesty the Queen and Prince Philip with Lord Aberconway, President of the R.H.S., and Lady Aberconway

6 April. Trusses showing. Tight buds.
13 April. Coming into flower.
15 May. Ripe already. Really concerned for danger of mildew.
18 May. Still a week to go . . .

A later diary shows her still full of anxiety, but more descriptive: '23 April. I am sitting on the tank in no 2, a silent house, no bees, no pollination possible, not a single bee, they cannot be flying in this cold.' And some days after she records: 'How I pray that pollination will have been adequate – all done by hand with a rabbit pad.'

Waterperry students of the day, who attended Chelsea in charge of the precious strawberries, remember being directed by their Principal to pay special attention to the Beekeepers Association in the Science Section.

The importance of science, with which may be included engineering, increased yearly – so much so, that in June 1962 the *Gardener's Chronicle* had a special article called 'The Scientists' Chelsea'. The National Institute of Agricultural Engineering that year showed improved methods of automatic watering for pot plants, later to be developed still more, to the great saving of time and labour. These were two commodities which seemed to become scarcer as the century advanced.

Another result of this trend was the increasing use of pot-grown plants. At the time this was often frowned on by professional gardeners, as an amusing but scathing article by Roy Elliott in a May 1964 issue of the *Gardener's Chronicle* shows. But the pot-plant became a permanent feature of the flower-lover's way of life, as space dwindled along with time and labour. Questions were asked at Chelsea, as to what to do with the pile of small pots which thus accumulated: and one suggestion given at the Enquiry Tent was to donate them to local garden guilds and welfare organizations. I know that this was often done, and that to the time of writing, small pots (preferably with earth in them) are very welcome at some old people's clubs.

1 April 1965 saw the reorganization of the London boroughs, in which many boroughs were swallowed up by their larger neighbours. Chelsea was a case in point, and the battle to keep its own name, even though it became part of the Royal Borough of Kensington, was bravely fought – and won. The fame of the Chelsea Show was not the least of the many reasons put forward for retaining the identity of this historic part of London, and one of the keenest campaigners was Mr Fred Hilsden, whose flower barrow at the corner of Wellington Square and the King's Road was the site of a mammoth petition during the months before amalgamation. And the name was saved – today it is the Royal Borough of Kensington *and* Chelsea.

In 1965 a College of Education was represented in the Scientific Section at Chelsea for the first time. This was Culham College, then a Teachers' Training College, which produced a study on *Mentha* (mint) with all its many varieties, and uses, illustrated and displayed. An added interest was that an article, 'Mints in Britain', referring to this Chelsea exhibit, in the *Gardener's Chronicle* of 29 May 1965, was written by Allen Paterson, who in 1973 was appointed Curator of the Physic Garden.

As the 1960s marched on, names of products appeared in a profusion, and with a regularity, unknown before.

Some had only recently been patented. In other cases, a name well known in one sphere now manufactured goods for use in another, such as British Celanese, who extended from making clothes and furnishing fabrics to producing cloches and tree-protectors. From the Dorset coast came nets and netting for gardening use, from the rope-making firm of Bridport-Gundry. (It may not be generally known that 'Bridport dagger' was the name for the hangman's rope once made by the firm. But happily this is not a subject for the story of the Chelsea Flower Show!)

The Sixties also saw the establishment of the Flower Arrangement Tent in all its splendour – and with its queues. In 1968 there were exhibits of floristry from commercial firms, as well as a different selection of amateur floral arrangements every day, which were the work either of individuals, or of clubs and societies all over the country. Lists of addresses of flower arrangement clubs were available in the Tent, and one Sussex club, and another in the Midlands, each doubled their membership in just one day.

New flowers and shrubs, new hybrids, new colours and scents, appeared every year – too many to recount. But there were disappearances too, and these casualties were mainly long-established gardening names – especially those which raised plants from seed. On the whole these firms still flourished, but the yearly triumphant journeys to Chelsea with glorious displays were over. As in the city streets the small trader was giving place to the supermarket, so in the gardening world the large Garden Centre was taking over as the place where everything needed for the garden could be seen and purchased in one spot. Previously seeds and some sundries had been available at hardware shops and florists, but the large nurseries sold almost exclusively to the trade, and to some very expert gardeners.

This popularization of gardening was a feature of the end of the Sixties, and the change and its implications will be discussed in the last chapter.

7

The Chelsea Flower Show is almost a world in itself. Though it lasts for less than a week, preparations for each new Show begin almost before the current year's exhibits are cleared away; and work continues simultaneously at desk and printing press, in laboratory and greenhouse, at home and abroad. In the actual Show grounds themselves, it is estimated that some 2,000 people are employed – both RHS and Royal Hospital staff, as well as those privately employed. But this number only refers to those connected with exhibits, stands and administration, and takes no account of the many 'services' there too. These have their own personnel, on whose efficient presence the well-being – and indeed the security – of the attending public depends.

Responsibility for everything connected with its tenancy of the Royal Hospital grounds lies with the RHS. This applies to the various necessary services, which then act according to those regulations which govern their own activities.

From their station in Lucan Place, the Chelsea Police have had responsibility for Show surveillance since 1965. Before that, the station at Gerald Road, Westminster, was responsible, but Chelsea police have always co-operated, since the very first Show in 1912. They have two separate sets of duties, those inside the Royal Hospital gates, and those outside.

Inside the Show, the police are invited to be there and are paid by the RHS for their presence. Policemen are not drafted to this job, they volunteer for it, and there is never any shortage of willing constables. In fact, it is the other way round – one policeman said it was regarded as the happiest of any extra duty asked for, and regretted that he personally had never had the luck to be on the Flower Show rota.

There are probably less than half a dozen uniformed men on duty inside the grounds, except on those days when Royalty visits – though the exact numbers, duties and hours vary from day to day, the first and last days being the most crowded. Over the years within memory, there have been few serious incidents, for the crowd is always happy and considerate. Pickpockets have been known, but rarely in recent years. In 1975 there were just two complaints made to the police, both of which were easily settled.

Though so few uniformed policemen are on duty inside the Show, some private security firms are employed, and retired policemen are also engaged through the Police Federation.

One of these men was Albert Bates, now eighty-five years old, who for years was on police duty at the House of Commons. He is very much a Chelsea man, and after retirement from the Police Force he sat as a Labour councillor on the old Chelsea Borough Council. He has vivid memories of the work he did at the Flower Show, on both night and day shifts. At one time he had to guard the strawberries, which always attract pilferers – but few got past ex-policeman Bates, and when he gave up his yearly watch, some strawberry exhibitors missed him badly. Albert Bates says his vigils were 'just another job', but as a Chelsea man he was always interested in so great an event in his 'home town', and he described the crowds as good-natured – unlike those at football matches or even sometimes at the House of Commons.

Outside the gates, the police have of course greater responsibility, mostly traffic control which grows more of a problem each year. The main object of the Chelsea police is to keep the traffic moving, and as far as possible to prevent the huge influx of visitors from upsetting local residents. Before the introduction of traffic wardens, meters, residents' parking and yellow lines, there used to be alterations in street directions. Many became 'one-way', so that it was quite a problem to find one's way home and to park outside one's own house. There were men (not police) to control – or try to control – parking. Local residents took their own precautions, and late in the evening before the Show opened, dustbins, chairs and other impedimenta would appear in front of some houses. Not that these were always successful – though once, when my dustbins had been removed and a car parked there instead, they were replaced in the evening with a note of thanks and a bunch of flowers on each. But other people were less fortunate, and sometimes there were angry altercations. Trouble, which did not penetrate the turnstiles, did erupt over parking in nearby streets. The strict parking regulations of today are not always popular, but for Chelsea residents they have proved their worth during Flower Show week.

Thursday of Show week is the main day for coaches – there were more than three hundred in 1975. All coach operators have to apply to Scotland Yard, and details are then sent to the Chelsea police. Exhibitors also require a great deal of parking space, and over the years a very good system has been evolved to cope with this. Exhibitors use sections of Battersea Park, and each section has a different coloured card to be displayed on the windscreen. Friday evening, when the Show closes at about five and there would normally be a rush to get away, is also controlled by these coloured cards, for each colour has its own time to cross to Battersea, and this must be strictly obeyed. The scheme works so well, that recently two officers who were planning transport operations for the Aldershot Tattoo, asked to be allowed to observe and copy.

The Automobile Association works with the police on traffic control. A hundred and ninety-four directions to the Show are put up within a radius of about five miles. These are placed in position on the Sunday before the Show, and taken down at the weekend after the Show ends. Inspector Harry Oxford has handled this job since 1968, and enjoys it, as he and many of his scouts take an active interest in the Show itself. Since the 'tidal flow' system was introduced on Albert Bridge, notices have also been put on this and other bridges to help traffic. One year AA scouts co-operated with police in a major traffic problem, when a water-main burst near the Show entrance.

There is always a fire risk when temporary buildings and large crowds are combined. The Greater London Council (and before that, the London County Council) have stringent fire regulations for all places of entertainment, though oddly enough the Chelsea Flower Show does not come under its aegis. But about ten years ago Mr I. Rodger of the RHS staff invited the Fire Prevention Unit to inspect preparations for the current Show, and since then this has been done annually, before the Show opens.

There are fire points, extinguishers and hoses in many places, as visitors will probably have noticed, though as far as anyone can remember, there has been no serious incident over the long years of the Show's existence. A minor incident did occur some time ago, when a cigarette end, carelessly tossed into a full container of waste, set it alight. But the size of the blaze can be judged by the fact that it was promptly extinguished – from a beer bottle!

The St John's Ambulance tent is fully equipped and manned during the whole period of the Show, as it has been since the very beginning. The tent is set up by the RHS, but is staffed by both men and women of the London District, all of whom (as is the case in every St John's Ambulance Post) are volunteers. They have given invaluable service over the years for a great variety of minor problems. Most frequent of these are small injuries, fainting, and grit or other foreign bodies in the eye.

Once a child swallowed a fruit stone. The stone's origin was not questioned, but one exhibitor had suspicions and little sympathy. Hardly any serious accidents have occurred. One St John's volunteer, many years ago, had to deal with a case of terrible sneezing and eye-watering. This was obviously hay-fever, and after a rest and the use of a whole box of tissues, the sufferer asked for advice. Though the volunteer, herself a keen gardener, hated to say it, the obvious suggestion was to keep away from the Chelsea – or any other – Flower Show. The advice was ignored, and the sufferer returned the next day, in further paroxysms of sneezing, but with her own tissues.

Toilets – only then the word had mercifully not been twisted to its present use – were in various discreet positions since the first Show of all, for men only. There is some controversy as to when facilities for women were first introduced. The RHS claims that these were first provided during the 1920s, whereas the Royal Hospital holds that this was not done until 1957. Nowadays, however, they are well distributed, equipped and sign-posted.

Electricity can be supplied to any part of the Show grounds, and is run off the Royal Hospital's own supply. I am informed that the complicated accountancy involved in payment for this is one of the major tasks of those dealing with the Show's financial affairs: the system evolved would beat that of even the most up-to-date computer. Water, very necessary in most aspects of the

Show, but above all to the existence of the flowers, is less complicated to supply and cost.

The drainage system is constantly revised, for this remains a problem. The posts of the great marquee are hollow, collecting water from the canvas 'valleys' above and channelling it into drains that run directly into the Thames.

The Post Office is set up in Main Avenue, and postage stamps can be bought there and telegrams dispatched. This has been the case since 1920, the second Show after the First World War. It is administered from the Chief Post Office in the South Western District, and is manned mostly by local staff. One of these said that it was essential to have very large stocks of stamps for foreign visitors, some of whom were disappointed that there was not a special postmark for the Show itself. Daily collections are made from the posting box there, though these (as is the case outside) grow fewer as the years go on! There are telephone booths near the Post Office and elsewhere in the grounds.

Also in Main Avenue, the Victoria branch of the National Westminster Bank has a stand. This branch, under various names, has been the Bank of the RHS since it began. It was in fact opened as the Victoria branch of the London & County Bank in 1805 – the year after the foundation of the RHS. The Bank at the Show is very busy, changing foreign currency and also changing larger English notes and coins – mainly into 2p pieces for the telephone. But the cashiers are often asked questions about purely horticultural matters, as happens at any post or stand in the Show grounds. The Bank did have a special link with the Show one year, when the Manager's wife won a coveted award in the Flower Arrangement competition.

Food at any fair or show is an object of particular interest, and sometimes a focus of criticism. As has been mentioned earlier, the food in the days of the Temple Shows had led to grumblings about litter and cooking smells. From the move to Chelsea in 1913 until the interruption of the First World War, Messrs Searcy, Tansley took over the catering, and did so very successfully. In 1923, the contract went to Messrs Joseph Lyons & Co (now Town and County Catering), who have held it ever since.

Though Chelsea is the Spring Show of the RHS, it ranks as a summer function, and salads and cold concoctions, with plenty of fruit and cream, have always seemed the right dishes to go with the floral glories all round. But as has been noted, the weather can be treacherous, and one elderly and regular visitor remembers the joy of occasional hot soups, such as Mulligatawny.

The caterers have a menu from 1923, when numbers were fewer and sit-down meals with waitress service were possible. As crowds grew, this had to be abandoned, and only the Press Luncheon Party and tea-parties can now be catered for in this way. In 1926 there was a Luncheon Marquee, run partly as a buffet and partly as a sit-down meal. The menu was delicious, including salmon mayonnaise, cold meat and chicken, salads, fresh fruit in liqueur, and cheeses. It was all written in French, but in English below it was stated that teas would be served from 3 pm.

The 1926 Wine List was varied, and its prices show the passage of time more clearly than anything else. A 1917

Claret, Château Duhart, was 7s 6d a bottle; a dry André Frères champagne was 13s; a measure of Scotch whisky was 1od and of gin 9d.

Messrs Lyons run a Ground Staff buffet for a fortnight before the Show, as well as during it. This includes breakfasts from quite an early hour. The now-familiar words 'Self-Service' began to appear, but there were also plenty of tables and seats, and exhibitors remember with pleasure the rest these provided, along with refreshment.

All waitress service, except for the Press Luncheon, had stopped with the last war and was never re-instated: several buffets under canvas appeared instead. 1955 saw an innovation – a Wimpy House. This was a log-cabin serving the Wimpy hamburger, which is now well known, but which then was a newcomer, having been introduced the previous year at the Ideal Home Exhibition. In 1963, buffet units were brought in which were mobile without appearing to be so, and confectionery stalls also appeared. Particularly popular with foreigners were those selling a variety of boiled sweets which the customer selected himself and put into a bag to be weighed.

Today, there is food supplied to suit every purse, even if there is a queue first. A great deal of thought is also given to the supplying and placing of garden tables and chairs, so that the food provided can be eaten in some degree of comfort.

The Press, and later radio and television, have played an important part in the Chelsea Show scene. There were forecasts and reports of each successive Show in national, regional, weekly and monthly journals – horticultural journals especially. Many leading European newspapers, particularly from Belgium, France and the Netherlands, sent special correspondents; and some came from even further afield.

But as well as merely reporting on the event, the Press often played a direct part at Chelsea. The *Daily Mail* Gold Cup of 1912 has already been mentioned – won by 'Madame Herriot', whose unusual colour (flame, salmon, cardinal, crimson, were among the conflicting adjectives used to describe it) caused good-natured controversy for some time in that paper's columns. A competition for the 'New *Daily Mail* Rose' was organized by Percy Thrower in 1973, and another was organized by Harry Wheatcroft in 1975. In 1921 and 1922, the *Daily Graphic* Cup for the best rock garden was offered.

From the outset, *The Times* treated the Chelsea Flower Show to leading articles, which often attracted correspondence, some of it critical. 1956 was a year when so much was written and spoken that it prompted comment from the then President of the RHS, Sir David Bowes-Lyon, at the Show's Press Luncheon. In particular, a *Times* special correspondent had visited a superb flower show held in Nantes, France, that April, and had written: 'The lasting impression is that the French are ahead of us in the production of horticultural spectacles, and your correspondent longs for the day when we in Britain can organize something like it.'

Newspapers occasionally also arranged for garden and group exhibits at the shows, especially *The Times*, the *Daily Express* and members of the horticultural press. In the 1970s the *Financial Times* arranged three very successful exhibits of a town garden, a suburban garden and a country garden, each appropriate to its setting.

Among the weekly journals, two stand out with superb reporting of the Flower Show, as well as illustrations and sometimes special supplements. These are *Country Life* and the *Illustrated London News* – a headline to an article on the 1920 Show in the latter was a quotation from Bacon: 'The Purest of Human Pleasures'.

The Pathé Newsreel, once an important and much appreciated part of cinema performances, reported on the Chelsea Flower Show in 1938, and then regularly after the war from 1947 until 1968. Mr H. C. Wynder, Librarian at the Pathé Film Library, writes: 'The form of presentations was for our newsreel to show the arrival of the Royal visitors, and follow them round the exhibition, and to record their fascination towards the display of flowers.' This was an excellent method of reporting, since, as has been mentioned, the Royal family is always well-informed and enthusiastic about horticulture.

The Chelsea Show was occasionally mentioned on the BBC's excellent gardening programmes before the last war, in the days when C. H. Middleton and Tom Hay made such a contribution. There was always a close link between the BBC and the RHS, a fact emphasized by Mr John Green, then Talks Controller of the BBC, at a Chelsea Press Luncheon in 1956. In 1947, the first post-war Flower Show was included in a programme called 'Picture Page', and was also mentioned on 'Woman's Hour', that same day, 21 May.

Now, with different television channels and brilliant colour, The Chelsea Show is brought annually to everybody's home, with all the fascination of its exhibits and of those inspecting them. It has also featured on various networks overseas. Belgium, that most flower-minded of countries, leads in this as might be expected. Recently it was pointed out that British television and radio gave nothing like equivalent coverage to the 'Floralies' at Ghent.

It may be added here that an additional service to Flower Show visitors, until a few years ago, were 'buskers', who entertained the queues outside the London Gate entrance. They were not encouraged by the police or the Show organizers, but were much enjoyed by the waiting visitors. One 'busker', very adept at a paper-tearing trick, used to hold up a many-petalled paper rose, and claim it would win a cup 'for sure, if allowed inside'.

With the dawn of 1970, and the approach of the new century, already a certain *fin de siècle* feeling had begun. A thousand years ago, Europe had awaited 1000 AD with dread: stars and prophesies foretold the end of the world. This was so much a matter of general belief that people in many countries stopped planning and planting and working, with the dreadful result, as the world went on, of famine and disease.

Armageddon is not anticipated in 2000 AD, though for many of us the world we knew is vanishing fast. Progress and the technological age means that some of us, in this country at least, are better fed, housed and educated than in previous years – and, thanks to the media and rapid communications, we are better informed about those places on the earth where it might almost still be 1000 AD.

But as environmentalists discovered how major scientific discoveries are threatening the earth's atmosphere and surface, the word 'ecology' appeared more and more often. The *Oxford Dictionary* defines it as 'a branch of biology dealing with living organisms' habits, modes of life and relations to their surroundings'. Ecology, and how to protect the earth from man-made diasasters, was discussed in books, in the Press, on the air, in lectures – and in the Chelsea Show catalogue. For 1970 was designated Nature Conservation Year, and in this the Chelsea Show played its part.

The Scientific Section in 1970 included a specially interesting display by the Parks and Botanic Gardens of the Corporation of Glasgow. The catalogue said: '. . . stress is laid on raising plants of species from seed – much of the seed having been collected in the wild. This work is considered of special importance from the conservation point of view, as the raising of rare and endangered species will bring into wider conservation plants which might be over-exploited or destroyed in their native habitat and thus lost to science. Botanic Gardens have an important part to play in the study and conservation of the world's flora, and in promoting an informed public opinion. . . .

Nearby, the Nature Conservancy Stand dealt with another aspect of this important question. Again from the 1970 Catalogue:

'Modern farming technology involving the destruction of hedges, copses, ponds and other wild life habitat, and the increased use of pesticides, has caused impoverishment of wild life in farmland. Urban expansion is encroaching on the countryside, reducing the area of farmland but producing new gardens which can go some way towards compensating for the loss of wildlife. If some of our native plants and animals can be accommodated in our gardens, this will contribute greatly to nature conservation in Britain.'

In 1973 the Nature Conservancy Act was passed, and Nature Conservancy as a unit merged into the Nature Conservancy Council, with three regional advisory committees, and a fourth committee on science. This is at Abbots Ripton, Huntingdon, which provided excellent exhibits at the Chelsea Flower Show in 1970, and in 1971.

The Department of the Environment was 'born' in 1970, with special responsibility for ecological problems. Although of course the Ministry of Agriculture is the department which has most contact with the RHS through its special committees, the Department of the Environment would also be more in touch as the years went on.

The first half of the 1970s saw an increase in scientific exhibits – mostly within the Science Section, naturally, but there were also some among the Garden Sundries, showing development in new materials and methods.

Colleges, which later developed into universities, and which had long-established botanic and horticultural departments, appeared year after year with new ideas and displays. The main ones were Long Ashton Research Station of Bristol University, the University of Reading, and Wye College of the University of London. And of course there are also the famous institutes – particularly Rothamsted at Harpenden, one of the earliest exhibitors of all, and John Innes at Norwich.

A comparative newcomer to Chelsea in the 1970s was its near neighbour, the Imperial College of the University of London, which is in Kensington. Professor A. J. Rutter, Head of the Department of Botany and Horticultural Technology in 1975, said he hoped that an exhibit could be mounted every other year, or thereabouts, as he regards it as an important exercise for students and staff alike. The difficulty is – and this goes for all university and college exhibits – that the Chelsea Show is perilously near examination time. In 1974, among other remarkable exhibits, the Imperial College had one aimed at assessing pollutants associated with motorways, and at finding resistants. This display was supported by the Transport and Roads Research Laboratory.

Among the most interesting stands in the Science Section was always that from the RHS Garden at Wisley, where questions answered ran into thousands. That of 1974, in particular, delighted both the skilled gardener and the amateur, for it dealt with a fairly new gardening interest – herbs. The small garden shown was stocked with plants of which roots, stems, leaves or flowers could be used in medicines, cooking or for perfume – as well as purely for decoration. Many exhibitors from the Flower Arrangement Tent were seen taking notes. In 1975 a new herb garden was opened at Wisley, which many who had seen the charming miniature in 1974 determined to visit.

Since the Show began there have been a few exhibits

from municipal organizations, but these increased greatly during the 1970s, and emphasized the importance of gardening in the cities. A collection of stocks of every colour and of delicious scent came one year from the Borough of Slough in Buckinghamshire; a Japanese garden was sent by the City of Liverpool; pelargoniums came from the London Borough of Hammersmith; a fine collection of flowering shrubs and trees journeyed up from the South Wight Borough Council in the Isle of Wight.

Many borough councils have sent greenhouse plants, most of them emphasizing different aspects of greenhouse growing. The City of Birmingham showed astounding greenhouse plants raised from seed; the Thurrock Borough Council in Essex sent plants grown with minimum heat; the London Borough of Hillingdon sent ornamental plants in vivid variety; and the London Borough of Havering concentrated on those with specially bright foliage.

Admiring details could be given of all these displays, but worth particular mention is the London Borough of Newham. This dockside area, once slum-land, now skyscraper-land, exhibited plants from as infinite a variety of conditions as can be imagined – a triumph of municipal horticulture and energy. Mr F. Hartwell, the 1975 Superintendent of the Parks and Recreation Section of this vast borough, is determined to see Newham represented at Chelsea again and again.

The 1975 Show brought some interesting developments, and, as the *Gardener's Chronicle* said, it 'weathered the weather', though lack of sun and cloudy skies proved disaster to some flowers. Roses suffered and so did sweet peas – all the sadder for these gentle flowers in that there had been no stand of them for a few years, and it was hoped for a fine display in 1975.

The 'Silver Lady', Pamela Underwood of Colchester, seemed yet again to have achieved a wider collection of her famous silver and grey foliage. Dazzling displays of fuchsias were presented this year, in wonderful combinations of red, white, mauve and pink, by Wills Fuchsia Nursery of West Wittering, Sussex, and by H. Woolman (Dorr) of Solihull. One old Chelsea Pensioner admiring them, was reminded of the year when a Pensioner had grown and sold a 'Busy Lizzie' as a new kind of fuchsia. 'He didn't know any better and nor did his customers,' he said. 'But we learn a lot every year at *our* Show.'

An exhibit which has appeared for years in sad simplicity is that of the Commonwealth War Graves Commission. Sir Fabian Ware was the pioneer of this idea, immediately after the First World War, and inspired a group of people to form the Commission and care for the graves of men and women in many countries. Yearly, relations of those so remembered come to this section of the Chelsea Flower Show to see the display which typifies what is being done elsewhere.

That garden commemorates the past: but the 1975 Show saw a stand which commemorated a very modern event – the Zaire River Expedition, which had followed the route of the explorer Stanley along the river then named the Congo. The stand in the Scientific Section, presented by Andrew Paterson and Dorothy Bovey (who took part in the expedition), showed botanical paintings and specimens of Zaire River flora and fauna.

1971 marked the fiftieth Chelsea Flower Show, and in the Press, around committee tables and in quiet conversations in private gardens, the future of the Great Spring Show of the RHS was discussed. It was becoming clearer every year that, as once the Temple Gardens had become overcrowded, so the Royal Hospital grounds were now facing the same problem. There was talk of a move to Birmingham where 310 acres had been earmarked for an Exhibition Centre – a municipal undertaking which has great local support, notably from the powerful Birmingham Chamber of Commerce. The question of a national Flower Show, on the lines of Belgium's 'Floralies', recurred once more.

Colin Parnell wrote an article in the *Gardener's Chronicle*, 21 May 1971, under the heading: 'What's Wrong with Chelsea?', in which he aired again the complaints and problems, such as restrictions and crowding, and lack of modern publicity. He suggested that the RHS should carry out a survey of the opinions of exhibitors and visitors. In fact, the exhibitors are asked regularly for their opinions, and on occasion the visitors have been asked whether Chelsea in its present form is what they want; the years have gone by, and the Flower Show remains remarkably the same in planning, appearance, and infinite charm. The immense Exhibition Centre in Birmingham was opened in February 1976 and will doubtless have Flower Shows as part of its imaginative programme. But the Great Spring Show of the RHS is very unlikely to be there – though some of its exhibitors may.

Peter Pashley, gardening correspondent of the *Birmingham Evening Post*, is sure that Chelsea has something to give in terms of prestige and enjoyment, which cannot be excelled. Where some are critical of shortage of space, he points out the advantage of this: when individual stands and displays are limited in size, exhibitors are spurred on to even greater efforts to ensure perfection of every bloom or leaf. Though ardent plantsmen always aim at perfection, having limited room makes it even more important that 'each flower should count every day, from the first to the last'.

Chelsea still ranks as one of the 'musts' in a changing social world. The old tea-parties have ended, but the list of visitors to the Show is still chronicled every year by the society correspondent, 'Jennifer', in *Harpers & Queen*. The roll call of names can be almost as interesting as the flowers displayed, for it shows the vast range of people who come to the Show, from home and abroad, from city and universities, from the social high-life of London and from the provinces.

Though inside the Royal Hospital grounds the glory of scent and colour, and the pleasure and interest of the visitors, remain the same, outside all is changing – and on those changes much of Chelsea's future depends. Chelsea's commercial importance has diminished since so many great firms no longer exhibit but rely more nowadays on mail order. With the growth of Garden Centres throughout the land, plant 'shopping' has become easier, and Chelsea visitors have been heard to say, often after a long examination at some stand and an even longer conversation with the attendant, 'Thank you. I'll go and get these from my Garden Centre'.

Lists are still handy, and often a pencil is lent, at every stand of flowers, fruit, vegetables and gardening sundries.

Orders are still placed – though one well-known nursery-man says they are often cancelled immediately afterwards. This attitude must be a disadvantage financially to a Chelsea exhibitor, but the growth of the Garden Centres as a whole is so good for gardening, and promotes so much interest, that things may balance themselves out in the end.

The fact that purchases cannot be made at the Show (except for some books and publications) has often been a subject for criticism. In 1975, the subject was being thoroughly discussed. It has obvious advantages, but difficulties as well: for already the harassed exhibitor must daily replace those plants which have wilted or passed their best, and to replace plants sold as well would be an added burden. But the views of all concerned are being consulted, and a decision will perhaps have been made even before this reaches print.

(Of course, as has already been mentioned, some plants are sold at the very end of the Show, but that is not quite the same thing.)

So the future is always uncertain, but much can be guessed and a little foretold. A ten years' lease was signed in 1975 between the RHS and the Hospital authorities. The Hospital has a new Governor, General Sir Antony Read, GCB, CBE, DSO, MC. The RHS has a new Secretary, John Cowell, MA. There is a new Superintendent of the Royal Hospital Grounds, J. W. Otterway. But these are human changes which do not break the continuity of more than sixty years of the Great Spring Show at Chelsea.

Louis Russell, of L. R. Russell Ltd, has immense confidence in the future of the Chelsea Show – a confidence which springs from experience (for his firm has exhibited since the beginning) and from a deep loyalty and affection for all that has made the Show what it is; a confidence which is shared by many of his profession.

But let the last word come from a member of the general public. 'Chelsea is the only show of any kind where you feel better when you come out than when you went in.'

Appendix

Awards at Chelsea Show

At the Show awards are given both to plants and exhibits (including gardens). Private or public gardeners or nurserymen may put up individual plants for award, whether they are on show elsewhere or not. All exhibits of plants and gardens are eligible for the award of a medal.

The RHS has several committees of experienced gardeners which meet regularly at all RHS Shows to judge exhibits and plants, and at Chelsea this judging is done on the afternoon and evening of the Monday before the Show opens. Judging the exhibits is a fairly tough job, physically as well as mentally, because the same class of exhibit is not grouped together and the committees have to go from one exhibit to another over the whole marquee. The judges are looking primarily for well grown plants or flowers, in the peak of condition, balanced growth and, with flowers, a high percentage fully open, neither in bud nor overblown.

The highest award for exhibits is the Gold Medal, and at Chelsea several are usually awarded – in 1975 thirty-one were given. The other medals available are given below in order of merit:

For exhibits of gardens, flowers and ornamental plants
The Society's Gold Medal
Silver-gilt Flora Medal
Silver Flora Medal
Silver-gilt Banksian Medal
Silver Banksian Medal
Floral Medal

For exhibits of fruit
The Society's Gold Medal
Silver-gilt Hogg Medal
Silver Hogg Medal
Hogg Medal

For exhibits of vegetables
The Society's Gold Medal
Silver-gilt Knightian Medal
Silver Knightian Medal
Knightian Medal

For exhibits of plants of special interest or beauty or showing exceptional skill in cultivation and for educational exhibits
The Society's Gold Medal
Silver-gilt Lindley Medal
Silver Lindley Medal
Lindley Medal

Plants are considered at separate meetings and come before one of the eleven committees that meet on Monday afternoon. Anybody can bring a plant that they think is a 'good garden plant' to show the committees, and it is considered by the Committee on its appearance at the meeting. Many of the plants are new, but others may have been grown in gardens for some time. These two groups are judged in the same way for their potential horticultural value, to include consideration of distinctiveness or any improvement over comparable plants already established, e.g. whether the shape has been improved or a new colour obtained by breeding.

The top award for plants is the First Class Certificate, 'for a plant of great excellence.' This is hardly ever given on the first appearance of a plant before the Committee; it is much more usual for plants to get this after they have achieved the next award, the Award of Merit. This is often given to older plants, but seldom to new flowers unless they have value as show (competition) flowers. The third award (the most cautious one) is the Certificate of Preliminary Commendation, which gives professional acknowledgement to exhibitors that their new baby is worth developing.

Index

Abbots Ripton, Nature
  Conservancy unit at, 135
Aberconway, Lady, 82, 116
Aberconway, Lord (Pres. of RHS
  1934–53), 95–7, 99, 100, 101,
  104–5, 116
Aberconway, Lord (Pres. of RHS
  1961–), 115–16
Aiton, William, 28
Aldenham gardens, 51, 71–2, 77,
  80
Aldenham, Lord, 35
Alexander, H. G., 112–13
Alexandra, Princess, 108
Allen, Mea, 61–2
Allwood, Messrs, 83, 89, 106
Allwood, Montagu C., 106
America, 39, 69–70, 74–5, 98–9
Amory, Rt Hon. D. Heathcote,
  106
Apples, 67, 79
Artificial flowers, 41
Associates of Honour (RHS), 77

Australia, 89
Automobile Association, 124–5
Awards and Medals, 14, 38, 78,
  97, 105, 143–5; Banksian Medal,
  17, 144; Cain Cup, 89; *Daily
  Graphic* Cup, 130; *Daily Mail*
  Gold Cup, 40; Flora Medal,
  144; Gold Medal, 96–7, 106,
  109, 116, 144; Hogg Medal,
  144; Knightsian Medal, 144;
  Lawrence Medal, 100; Lindley
  Medal, 29, 113, 145; Sherwood
  Cup, 77, 88, 89, 92, 93; Silver
  Jubilee Cup, 85–6; Sutton
  Vegetable Cup, 88; Veitch
  Memorial Medal, 21, 91;
  Victoria Medal of Honour, 76,
  91, 115; Westonbirt Orchid
  Medal, 112–13
Azaleas, 12, 86, 89, 100

Baker, D. A., 106
Banks, Sir Joseph, 16–17, 27–8

Barnes, Nicholas, 35
Barr and Sons, Messrs, 93
Bartlett, C., 85–6
Bates, Albert, 123
BBC Television and Radio, 109,
    131
Beck, Ellen, 45
Beckett, Edwin, 34–5, 51, 71–2,
    77, 79, 80, 86
Bee Research Association, 113
Beekeepers Association, 117
Begonias, 81, 92
Belgium, 58, 59–60, 82, 100;
    'Floralies' at Ghent, 14, 36, 101,
    114, 132, 139
Bentley, Thomas, 19
Birmingham, City of, 137, 139
Birmingham Evening Post, 139
Black and Flory, Messrs, 88
Blackcurrant sawfly, 114
Blackmore and Langdon, Messrs,
    of Bath, 92
Blackwell, Elizabeth, 18, 19
Bodnant Garden, Wales, 82, 96, 105
Bolton, H., and Son, 88
Bolton, J. H., 106
Borough Council displays, 137
Boulestin, Marcel, 76
Bovey, Dorothy, 138
Bowes-Lyon, Hon. Sir David,
    105, 108, 114–15, 130
Bridport-Gundry, Messrs, 119
British Celanese, 119
British Gardeners' Association, 42
Brown, 'Capability', 16
Bull, A. J., Chelsea contractors, 84
Bull, Edward, 61
Bull's Nurseries, 60–1
Bunyard, G., of Maidstone, 79
Buskers, 132

Cacti and desert plants, 75
Cain Cup, 89
Camellia Conference, 101
Capek, Karel, 71
Carnations, 82–3, 89, 106; *Robert
    Allwood*, 83
Cartwright, Walter, 37–8, 39, 40,
    102

Catalogues (of Show), 40, 41, 55,
    56, 60, 71, 82, 134–5
Catering, 48, 74, 128–9
Charlton Fair, Kent, 24
Cheadle Mental Hospital, 88
Chelsea China Works, 19, 73
Chelsea Gardens Guild, 26
Chelsea Pensioners, 23, 39, 58, 138
Chelsea Tea-parties, 73–4
Chillianwallah Monument, 24, 49,
    52
Clematis, 15, 69–70
Clements, Julia (later: Lady
    Seton), 98–9
Cloches, 55, 119
Coaches, 124
Colman, Sir Jeremiah, 34, 113
Colquhoun, Tommy, 60
Commonwealth War Graves
    Commission, 138
Country Life, 131
Country Matters (Leighton), 25
Cowell, John, 141
Coxhead, Elizabeth, 90
Crown Estate Commissioners, 100
Cucumbers, 61–2
Culham College, 118
A Curious Herbal (Blackwell), 18
Cymbidiums, 86

Daily Express, 130
Daily Graphic Cup, 130
Daily Mail Gold Cup, 40, 130;
    'New *Daily Mail* Rose'
    competition, 130
Dalrymple, Lord, 59
Dartington Hall Garden
    Department, 83
Dean, G. C. T., 46
Dean's Shreds, 55
Delphiniums, 11, 92, 104; Blue
    Tomtit, 116
Department of the Environment,
    135
Deposits (paid by exhibitors), 54
Dickson, Alex, Messrs, 88
Dickson, James, 28
Donald, General C. J., 58

Dunnett, W. H., 106

East Malling Research Station, 113
Edward, Prince of Wales, (later:
    Edward VIII/Duke of Windsor),
    75, 83-4, 105
Electricity supply, 83, 126
Elizabeth, Queen, the Queen
    Mother, 19, 75, 88, 115
Elizabeth II, Queen, 102, 103, 108
Elliot, Roy, 117
Empire Exhibit (1937), 88-9
Empire Exhibition, Wembley
    (1924), 71
Enquiry and Literature Stands, 12,
    60, 66, 101, 118
Escoffier, Maître-Chef, 113

Federation of Women's Institutes,
    66
Fellows' Day, 14-15, 80-1, 91, 100
Ferdinand, Archduke of Austria,
    42-3
Festival of Britain, 101-2
Fielder, C. R., 35
Fife, John, 107
Fifth International Botanic
    Congress, Cambridge (1930), 75
Financial Times, 130
Findlay, R., 85, 89
Fire precautions, 125
First Aid Tent, 12, 125-6
First World War (1914-18),
    56-63, 64, 96, 138
Fletcher, H. R., 111
'Floralies' at Ghent, 14, 36, 82,
    101, 132, 139; Quinquennial of,
    114
'Floriade' at Rotterdam, 114
Fletcher, Dr H. R., 33, 104-5
Flower Arrangement, 90, 97-9,
    119, 136
Flower Decoration and Flowers in
    House and Garden (Spry), 90
Foreign exhibits, 14, 39, 40, 74-5,
    76, 89, 100, 103, 108-9
Forsyth, William, 27-8
Fort Belvedere, Sunninghill, 83-4
Fortune, Robert, 110

4th Battalion Royal Fusiliers, 51
Fowler, J. Gurney, 33-4, 38
France, 14, 39, 40, 58, 60, 108-9,
    130
Fruit, 12, 15-16, 24, 39, 55, 61,
    63, 66-7, 76, 77-8, 79, 80, 92,
    99, 101, 108-9
Fuchsias, 15, 138

Garden Centres, 119-20, 140-1
Garden Club Journal (RHS), 37
Garden furniture, 12, 41
'The Garden of Tomorrow' (The
    Times exhibit, 1959), 109
Gardener's Chronicle, 29, 32, 34, 35,
    49, 53, 58-9, 60, 67, 69-70, 78,
    87, 92-3, 96, 97, 106, 107, 109,
    115, 117, 118, 137-8, 139
The Gardener's Dictionary (Miller),
    18, 19
Gardener's Magazine, 36, 55, 70
Gardeners' Royal Benevolent
    Institution, 78
Gaskell Mr (Asst. Secretary of
    RHS), 38
Gatton Park, nr Redhill, 34, 113
General Strike (1926), 72
Genus Rosa (Willmott), 76
George V, King, 36, 37, 53, 69,
    75, 76, 84, 86-7
George VI, King, 75, 88, 102
Germany, 14, 39
Gibbs, Hon. Vicary, 35, 51, 71,
    77, 80
Glasgow Corporation Parks and
    Gardens display (1970), 134
Glasshouse Crops Research
    Institute, 114
Gloucester, Duke of, 89
Gloxinias, 92
Grand National Rose Show,
    First (1858), 25-6
Grape vines, 15-16, 76
Grass Gardens, 69
Green, John, 131
Greenhouses, 12, 83, 114, 137
Greenwood, Hubert, 35
Grenfell, Field Marshal Lord, 53
Greville, Hon. Charles, 28

Ground Staff canteen, 129
Gwynn, Nell, 23

Hales, William, 91
Hamilton, Dr Lilias, 56
Hammersmith Borough Council, 137
Hanbury, Sir Cecil, 91
Hanbury, Frederick Janson, 35
Hanbury, Sir Thomas, 91
Hanger, F., 85, 89, 116
Hans Sloane Flowers (China), 19
Hartwell, F., 137
Havergal, Beatrix, 55, 92, 116–17
Havering Borough Council display, 137
Hay, Roy, 108–9
Hay, Thomas, 104
Hays, Tom, 131
Henry VIII, King, 16
Herbaceous plants/border, 11, 51
Herbs, herb gardens, 64, 76–7, 136
Hibbert, George, 20
Hill, Captain, 55–6
Hill, Jason, 76
Hillier, H. G., 107
Hillingdon Borough Council display, 137
Hilsden, Fred, 118
Hole, Rev. Samuel Reynolds, Dean of Rochester, 25
Holford, Sir George, 112
Holland, 39, 114
Holland, Henry, 16
Honeysuckle (*Banksia*), 16–17
Hope-Nicholson, Mrs, 73
Horse boots, 71
Horticultural Colour Chart (RHS), 92, 97
Horticultural Record of the Royal International Horticultural Exhibition of 1912, 53
Horticultural Training Centres for Women, 55, 56
Hortus Veitchii (Veitch), 21
Hoyt, A. Sherman, 74–5
Hudson, James, 35

Illustrated London News, 131
Imperial Botanical Conference, S. Kensington (1930), 75
Imperial College display, 136
Imperial Horticultural Conference (1930), 75
Ingwersen, Will, 116
Inheritance in Potatoes, (Salaman) 41
Inner Temple Benchers, RHS shows in grounds of (1888–1911), 29–32, 33, 49, 139
Insect research, 113–14
International Flower Show, New York (1947), 99

Jaby, G. N., 71
Jackman, A. G., 35
Jackman, G. and Co., 69
Jams and pickles, RHS booklet on, 66
Janes, E. R., 99
Japan, 14, 39, 106
Japanese garden, 137
Jekyll, Gertrude, 76
Jewson, Mrs Anne, 50
John Groom's Flower Girls Mission, 41
John Innes Horticultural Institute, Norwich, 93, 136

Kew, Royal Botanic Gardens at, 82, 88–9, 103, 109–10, 114
Killerton Nurseries, Nr Exeter, 21
King, William, 73
Knight, F. P., 107
Knight, Joseph, 20
Knight and Perry Nurseries *see* Veitch Nurseries

Lambourne, Lord, 68
Langdon, Allan, 107
Lawn-mowers, 71; radio-controlled, 109
Lawrence, Sir Trevor, 42, 52–3
Lawrence Medal, 100
Laxton, Messrs, 70, 79
Leach, John, 26
Leighton, Clare, 25
Lilies, 81

Lindley, John, 29
Lindley medal, 29, 112
Lister, Bella, 112
Liverpool, City of, 137
Lobjoit, Sir W., 66–7
London Gardens Gift Scheme, 97
Long Ashton Research Station,
  Bristol University, 135
Love-in-the-Mist, 77
Lovelace, Lady, 73
Lupins, 15; Russell, 89
Luttrell, Narcissus, 16
Lycett, Brigadier C. V. L., 102
Lyceum Club, 56
Lyons, Joseph, and Co., 128, 129

Macdonald and Sons, 69
McKeller, A., 35
Maclaren, Hon. H. D. (later
  Lord Aberconway), 82
Manor of Chelsea, 17
Marquee(s), 13–14, 49, 61, 77,
  102, 126
Mary, Queen, 69, 73, 84, 86–7, 104
Mason, C. E., 88
Maude, Cyril, 71
Men of the Trees, 93
Mendip Nurseries, 55–6
Middleton, C. H., 131
Miller, Philip, 18, 19
Mint (Mentha), 118
Model gardens, 79
'Mops' fair, Marlborough, 24
More, Thomas, 16
Morgan, Howard, 55–6
Munro, George, 66
Music (at Shows), 41, 52, 60, 62

National Association of Flower
  Arrangement Societies of Great
  Britain, 98
National Farmers' Union stand
  (1948), 99
National Institute of Agricultural
  Engineering, 117
National Rose Society, 26, 104;
  Silver Jubilee of (1936), 88
National Westminster Bank, 12,
  127–8

Nature Conservancy (1970), 134–5
New Zealand, 77, 89
Newham Borough Council
  exhibits, 137
Ninth International Horticultural
  Congress, Caxton Hall (1930),
  75

Occupational Centre for the
  Unemployed, 78
Oeshoven, M. van, 60
Olivier, Sydney, 17–18
Onions and root vegetables, 71–2
Otterway, J. W., 141
Orchids, 12, 21, 33, 47, 49, 53, 62,
  78–9, 85–6, 88, 111–13, 115;
  Bee, 111; Lycaste Skinneri, 113;
  Miltonias and Cattleyas, 88;
  Westonbirt Medal, 112–13
Orchids and Their Cultivation
  (Sander), 112
Oxford, Harry, A.A. Inspector, 124

Page, Russell, 108
Parking, 123–4
Parnell, Colin, 139
Pashley, Peter, 139–40
Paul, Messrs, of Waltham Cross,
  58
Paterson, Allen, 118
Paterson, Andrew, 138
Pathé Newsreel, 131
Payne, C. Harman, 35
Pearson, R. Hooper, 35
Pelargoniums, 137
Pensioner-gardeners, 107
Perfect, B. F., 34, 113
Pernet, M., 40
Pershore Midsummer Fair, 24
Physic Garden, Chelsea, 17, 18,
  19, 28, 29, 47, 91, 110, 118
Pictures of flowers and gardens
  (exhibited at Show), 73
Piggot Brothers of Ongar, 14, 102
Pinks, garden or Granny's, 89,
  99
Plant containers, 41
Police, 122–4
Pope, Mary, 99

Portland, Duke of, 33
Post Office, 12, 127
Pot plants, 117–18
Potager, French, 108–9
Potatoes, 66, 114
Press, 68, 78, 109, 129–31;
  Luncheon, 101, 106, 128, 129,
  130, 131
Primeurs, 105
Primula helodoxa, 39
Primulas, 74
Private View, 14–15, 80–1, 91,
  100
Puddle, Mr, 96–7

Queen Mary's Garden, Regent's
  Park, 104

Radio and Television coverage,
  109, 129, 131–2
Ranelagh Gardens, 22–3, 49, 69,
  109
Read, General Sir Anthony, 114
Reading University, 135
Redlap Gardens, 71
Refreshments, 14, 30, 42, 60, 62,
  69, 110, 128–9
Rhododendron Conference (1949),
  101
Rhododendrons, 12, 20, 81, 84,
  85–6, 91–2, 96–7, 100, 101, 105,
  106; *Yakushimanum*, 106
Rivers, T., & Sons, 79
Robots (Capek), 71
Rock and water gardens, 14, 40,
  50, 62, 65, 83–4, 96; *Daily
  Graphic* Cup for best, 130
Rodgers, I., 125
Rose(s), 11, 25–6, 58, 62, 70, 76,
  81, 88, 104, 137; dwarf
  Polyanthus, 88; 'Mme Edouard
  Herriot, the *Daily Mail* Rose',
  40, 130; moss, 16; 'New *Daily
  Mail* Rose' competition, 130;
  scarlet rambler, 58; Wheatcroft,
  88
Rothamsted Experimental
  Station, 114, 136
Rothschild, Leo de, 35, 39

Rothschild, Lionel de, 81, 85–6,
  89
Royal Artillery Band, 52
Royal Exotic Nurseries *see* Veitch
  Nurseries
Royal Gardeners' Benevolent
  Institution, 107
Royal Gardeners' Orphan Fund, 78
Royal Horticultural Society
  (RHS), 12, 13, 19; Association
  of Honour of, 77; Fellows' Day
  (Private View), 14–15, 80–1, 91,
  100; Flower Shows held in
  Inner Temple (1888–1911),
  29–32; founding and
  development of, 27–32; Fruit-
  growing Conference (1919),
  66–7; membership and
  subscriptions, 28, 57, 95;
  Orchid Committee, 33; Red
  Cross Sale (1916), 62;
  Sesquicentenary of (1953), 103,
  105, 115; Vincent Square HQ,
  29, 57, 64, 106; *see also* Wisley
Royal Horticultural Society:
  Chelsea Flower Shows;
  Summer Show (1905), 33;
  Spring Shows: 1913: 13, 32,
  48–52; 1914: 54–5; 1915: 58–9,
  60; 1916: 61–2; 1919: 64–6;
  1920: 68; 1921: 69; 1922:
  69–70; 1924: 71; 1925: 71–2;
  1926: 72–3; 1929: 74; 1930:
  76–8; 1931: 78–80, 81; 1932:
  78, 80–3; 1933: 82–3; 1934:
  83–4; 1935: 84–6; 1936: 87–8;
  1937: 88–90; 1938: 91–2; 1939:
  92–3; 1947: 96–7; 1948: 97–8,
  99–100; 1949: 100–1; 1950:
  101; 1951: 101–2; 1952: 102–3;
  1953: 103; 1954: 105; 1955:
  105; 1956: 106; 1957: 106–7;
  1958: 108–9; 1959: 109–10;
  1960: 111; 1961: 113; 1962:
  113; 1970: 134–5; 1971: 135,
  139; 1974: 136; 1975: 137–8
Royal Hospital, Chelsea, 12, 13,
  22; founding of (1683), 23–4;
  Royal International

151

Royal Hospital, Chelsea—*cont.*
  Horticultural Exhibition held in
  grounds of (1912), 32–43; *see
  also* RHS
Royal Hospital, Chelsea, The (Dean),
  46
Royal International Horticultural
  Exhibition (1912), 14, 31,
  32–43, 45, 49, 53, 76, 79, 84
Russell, Louis (L. R. Russell
  Ltd), 141–2
Rutter, Prof. A. J., 136

Sabine, Joseph, 28
St John's Ambulance Tent, 125–6
St Paul's Waldenbury gardens,
  Herts., 75
Salaman, Dr Radclyffe, 40–1
Salisbury, Richard Anthony,
  19–20, 28
Sander, David, 112
Sargent, R., 106
Savill, Sir Eric, 100
Schröder, Baron, 78
Scientific and education Section/
  exhibits, 12–13, 40, 66, 69, 93
  113–14, 117, 118, 134–6, 138
Sealed Orders (Raleigh and Hamil-
  ton) 52
Seaman, Owen, 62
Searcy Tansley, Messrs, 48, 128
Second World War, 59, 95, 96, 98
Security (at Shows), 12, 51, 121,
  122–3
'Self-folding Chelsea Imperial'
  (Cos lettuce), 21
Services at Shows, 121–9
Shaftesbury House, 16
Shailer, Mr, lavender grower, 16
Sherwood Cup, 77, 88, 89, 92, 93
Shirley poppies, 46
Siam, King and Queen of, 84
Silver Jubilee celebrations (1935),
  84–6
Silver Jubilee Cup, 85–6
Silver-leaved foliage, 99, 138
Simmonds, A., 102
Sloane, Sir Hans, 17–18, 19
Slough Borough Council display

of stocks, 137
Slug traps, 55–6
Smilax, 57
Smollett, Tobias, 22
Sociedad de Amigos del Paisaje y
  Jardines de Madrid, 102
Society for the Improvement of
  Horticulture, 28; *see also* RHS
Society of Apothecaries, 17, 28
Soil sterilization by electric power,
  83
South African exhibits, 76, 89
South Wight Borough Council
  display, 137
Spanish garden, 102–3
Spraying, uses of, 66
Spry, Constance, 90, 98
Stevenson, Violet, 99
Stocks, 137
Stone figures, 69
Stove Plants, 41
Strawberries, 12, 66, 70, 79;
  Waterperry, 55, 92, 116–17
Streeter, Fred, 86
Strong, Sir T. Vezey, Lord Mayor
  of London, 34
Sundries, Garden, 12, 64, 79, 82,
  90, 135
Sutton, Arthur, 35
Sutton, D. Noel, 107
Sutton, Leonard, 80
Sutton's displays ('Sutton's
  Circus'), 51–2, 80, 82, 99
Sutton Vegetable Cup, 88
Sweeting, Edward, 101
Sweet-peas, 11, 65, 88, 137–8

Table decoration, 57, 90
Tannock, David, 77
Thatcham Horticultural School
  for women, 55
Third World Orchid Conference
  (1960), 111, 115
Thrower, Percy, 130
Thurrock Borough Council
  display, 137
The Times, 108–9, 130; 'The
  Garden of Tomorrow' exhibit
  of, 109

Titchmarsh, C. C., 37–40, 42–3, 76, 102
Toilets, 126
Tom's Weeds (Allen), 61
Tonbridge, Alderman George, Mayor of Chelsea, 100
Torquay Wheelbarrow, 71
Traffic control, 123–5
Transport and Roads Research Laboratory, 136
Tulips, 11, 25, 42, 84, 93

Underwood, Pamela ('The Silver Lady'), 99, 138

Vanderlinden, M., 100
Vegetables, 12, 21, 23, 35, 39, 51–2, 55, 61–2, 63, 64, 66, 71–2, 77, 80, 88, 99, 101, 105, 108–9, 114
Veitch family, 20–2, 113
Veitch, Sir Harry, 22, 33, 36, 47, 51, 53
Veitch, James, 'the younger', 21
Veitch, James H., 20, 36
Veitch, John, 21
Veitch Memorial Fund, 36
Veitch Memorial Medal, 21, 91
Veitch Nurseries (Royal Exotic Nurseries), 20–1, 60–1
Victoria Medal of Honour (VMH) 76, 91, 115
Vilmorin-Andrieux, 108

Wallace, R. W., of Colchester, 53
Walpole, Horace, 22–3
War Horticultural Relief Fund, 59
Ward, Dr Nathaniel, 110
Wardian Case, 110
Ware, Sir Fabian, 138
Water supply, 126–7
Waterer, Messrs, 20
Waterperry Horticultural School for women, 92, 116
Wattles (mimosa), 89

Webb, Arthur, 67
Wedgwood, John, 19, 27–8
Wedgwood, Josiah, 19
Welsh, Alderman Frederic, Mayor of Chelsea, 47–8, 50
Westonbirt Orchid Medal, 112–13
Wheatcroft, Harry, 107, 130
White, Edward, 35, 79
Whitelegg, George C., 109
Whitelegg, Harold G., 107
Wilks, Rev. W., 31, 45, 64
Willmott, Ellen Ann, 76
Wills Fuchsia Nursery of West Wittering, 138
Wimpy House, 129
Windsor, Duke of *see* Edward Prince of Wales
Windsor Great Park, Savill Garden, 100
Wisley, RHS Garden at, 12, 18, 35, 37, 65, 69, 91, 102, 106, 116, 136
Wisley Garden Endowment Trust Fund, 65
Wistaria, 49
Wister, John C., 69–70
Woking Nurseries, 35
Women gardeners/florists, 55, 56, 66, 92, 97–8
Women's Voluntary Service (now WRVS), 97
Wood, William, and Sons Ltd, 103,
Woolley, R. V. Gifford, 79–80
Woolman, H. (Dorr), of Solihull, 138
Wren, Sir Christopher, 13, 23
Wright, S. T., Superintendent of Wisley, 35
Wright, 'Bandsman' E., 41
Wye College, 113–14, 135
Wynder, H. C., 131

Zaire River Expedition display, 138